Create Your Own KidLab:

TIPS AND IDEAS TO MAKE SCIENCE ENGAGING, IMAGINATIVE, AND FUN

THIRD BOOKLET IN THE "BY TEACHERS, FOR TEACHERS" SERIES

THIS BOOK WAS DEVELOPED BY THE PROFESSIONAL EDUCATORS OF
THE NEIGHBORHOOD HOUSE CHARTER SCHOOL

KEVIN EMERSON

WITH

MELISSA BASQUIAT, LEAH BLAKE, LAURA FIELDS, ANNE KNIGHT, KATE NISSENSON

PUBLISHED BY THE PROJECT FOR SCHOOL INNOVATION

KEVIN ANDREWS AND MICHAEL ROTHMAN, CO-FOUNDERS

THE PROJECT FOR SCHOOL INNOVATION IS AN INITIATIVE OF THE
NEIGHBORHOOD HOUSE CHARTER SCHOOL. PUBLICATION OF
THIS BOOKLET WAS SUPPORTED BY GRANTS FROM THE
MASSACHUSETTS DEPARTMENT OF EDUCATION AND THE
NEW ENGLAND BIOLABS FOUNDATION.

EDITED BY MICHAEL ROTHMAN

ADDITIONAL DEVELOPMENT BY EMILY PRATT

DESIGN BY CHRIS BEBENEK

ILLUSTRATIONS BY KEVIN EMERSON AND ELIZA JONES

COVER BY LUKAS HAUSER

Answer Twenty Questions and You Could Win a Prize!

We value your feedback. In return, we'll put your name in a raffle to receive free technical assistance on KidLab (value: $150) or a $150 gift certificate from Barnes & Noble.

Pick One:

❑ Put me in a raffle to receive free technical assistance from an expert PSI teacher on KidLab.
❑ Put me in a raffle to receive a $150 gift certificate redeemable at any Barnes & Noble bookstore.
❑ Don't put me in either raffle. I'm suspicious of door prizes.

Personal Information

PSI will not share your personal information with any mailing lists without your permission.

Name_____ E-mail_____
Address_____

1. Age: 18-24   25-30   31-40   41-50   51+

2. Which best describes the area where you work?
Inner-city   Suburban
Urban   Rural

3. If you work with children, approximately how many are low-income, according to federal guidelines?
0-10%   25-50%   75-100%
10-25%   50-75%

If you work in a school:

4. How long have you been working in schools?_____

5. What is your position?
Classroom teacher   Administrator   Other_____
Specialist   Therapist

6. If applicable, what grade level(s) do you work with most?

7. If applicable, what subject area(s) do you work with most?

If you do not work in a school:

8. What is your occupation?_____

9. In what capacity (if any) do you work with teachers or schools?_____
_____

Please rate the statements below on a scale of 1-5: 1-Strongly Agree, 2-Agree, 3-Neither Agree Nor Disagree, 4-Disagree, and 5-Strongly Disagree.

10. The information in this booklet was presented in a way that made it easy to understand.　　　　1　2　3　4　5

11. The information presented in this booklet appeared credible.　　　　1　2　3　4　5

12. The fact that this booklet was written "by teachers, for teachers" was important to me.　　　　1　2　3　4　5

13. Overall, what I got out of this booklet was worth the time I put into it.　　　　1　2　3　4　5

14. This booklet has given me ideas that I will be able to take back to my classroom, school, or place of work.　　　　1　2　3　4　5

14a. If you agreed to the above statement, what were the two or three most valuable ideas? If you disagreed, why did you disagree?

15. How would you say this booklet compares to other publications you've seen on education practices?
Much Better　　Somewhat Better　　About the Same　　Somewhat Worse　　Much Worse

16. I would recommend that my colleagues look at this booklet.　　Yes　　　　No

17. Why or why not?

18. Your comments are valuable to us. Please provide any other useful thoughts:

19. Learn more about KidLab!
❏ Yes! Please tell me about how to apply for training on KidLab.
❏ Yes! Please tell me about other ways to receive technical assistance on KidLab.
❏ No. I would rather not learn more about KidLab at this time.

20. Learn more about the Project for School Innovation
❏ Yes! Please send me information about PSI by e-mail (preferred).
❏ Yes! Please send me information about PSI by postal mail.
❏ Yes! Please add me to the PSI mailing list to receive regular updates about PSI.
❏ No. I would rather not learn more about PSI at this time.

The Project for School Innovation

The Project for School Innovation was founded in 2000, in the midst of growing demand for education reform. PSI's founders felt that with repeated calls for improvement in public schools, the "professional expertise" in education was too often seen as coming from outside schools: from researchers, consultants, or business leaders. While such outsiders certainly have much to offer, PSI was founded on the belief that there is significant professional expertise inside every public school in this country—expertise that needs to be identified and shared. PSI was developed to recognize and highlight the expertise of teachers, administrators, and staff by facilitating reflection and collaboration on effective practices at public schools.

The How-To Guides by Teachers, for Teachers

Create Your Own KidLab: Tips and Ideas on How to Make Science Engaging, Imaginative, and Fun is the third in a series of how-to guides developed "By Teachers, For Teachers" with support from the Project for School Innovation.

Each guide produced by PSI is based on the work of professional educators at a PSI member public school. Through a year-long process, PSI works with these teachers to identify an effective practice, explore and document what makes this practice work, and offer tips and ideas for others to learn from their experience. Before a booklet is completed, the ideas in that booklet have been tested through the development of an action plan at other public schools looking to adopt the effective practice. By tracking the progress schools make with their action plans, we are able to further elucidate the transferability and replicability of the ideas presented here.

Our goal is to provide the information and ideas that will be useful to other teachers who want to try to bring these innovative practices to their own schools. The guides have been designed to be easy to use and reflect not just *theories* that are being proposed, but *practices* that have been developed, used, and tested by teachers, for teachers in public schools.

Training and Technical Assistance

Effectively adopting a new practice and adapting it to a school, classroom, or other learning environment requires more than reading one booklet. PSI offers training and technical assistance from the same teachers and staff who developed the practice you are reading about here. In addition, PSI offers technical assistance to make organizational change succeed.

If you would like to do more with the ideas you read about in this booklet, contact PSI to find out what training and technical assistance are available. In many cases scholarships are also available to defray some or all of the costs involved.

project for school innovation
A Neighborhood House Initiative

197A Centre Street
Dorchester, MA 02124

Tel: 617-825-0703 x.246
Fax: 617-825-1829
E-mail: PSI@teacher.com

http://www.psinnovation.org

project for school innovation
A Neighborhood House Initiative

THE FOUR CORE BELIEFS OF THE PROJECT FOR SCHOOL INNOVATION

1. Recognition for Strengths

Every school should be recognized for its *strengths*, and every school should be helped to address its *needs*.

2. Respect for Educators

No one knows how to do this better than the *professional educators* – teachers, administrators, and staff – who are engaging in the work of successful education reform *every day*.

3. The Responsibility to Share

If public education in America is truly to *serve all children*, then every public school has the responsibility to *share* its successful practices with others.

4. Tools for Change

Every school is unique, but every school can also learn from others, if it has the *tools,* the *support,* and the *leadership* to help make that happen.

Table of Contents

What is KidLab?

ASK SOMEONE WHAT IS UNIQUE ABOUT NEIGHBORHOOD HOUSE CHARTER SCHOOL AND, WITHOUT FAIL, THEY WILL BRING UP KidLab. KidLab is a little like a classroom and a little like a museum; it is a little like a laboratory and a little like an art studio. It is a little like all of these but unlike any of them. Inside KidLab, children learn to make connections between science, nature and art by working on hands-on, minds-on projects. KidLab is a place for discovery and exploration. It is also a place where real artwork and real science can be accomplished and evaluated. Children experience their learning about science and art directly. They make paintings and design experiments. They watch frogs and write stories. By combining different academic themes in KidLab, students can apply and extend the learning that goes on during their regular classroom day. By making real-life information and real-life tools available, children have a chance to work on real-world problems, formulate solutions and be taken seriously for their efforts.

Like a CLASSROOM...

KidLab is a safe, enriching environment where students learn. Teachers and children come together to ask questions, take risks, do important work, and increase their skills and knowledge.

Like a MUSEUM...

KidLab is driven by the needs and the interests of those who spend time in it. Students learn to interact with exhibits, displays, materials, and each other in a responsible, serious fashion so that they may understand what they encounter on a deep level.

Like a LABORATORY...

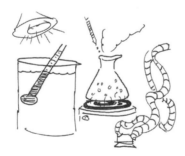

KidLab supports an atmosphere of scientific research and collaboration. Children are given time and space to study the world in a scientific manner. They must, of course, also determine what doing science is all about, and through daily experiences with the difficulties and rewards of scientific work, they will.

Like an ART STUDIO...

KidLab is a place where creative expression is encouraged. Students are reminded that everyone is an artist, capable of producing exciting, meaningful artwork. With many different media, children discover their artistic voice, and practice using it.

a DAY in the LIFE of KidLab

The otherworldly entryway is an important part of KidLab, giving students the feeling that they are entering a place both unique and familiar.

It is Thursday, and every student in Ms. Knight's third grade class knows what that means: It is KidLab day. At nine o'clock, half the class gets up from their chairs and tables and walks across the hall, where they are transported to a whole different world.

On the door of KidLab are photographs of students from years of KidLab projects, so that the fifth graders see their friends from third grade and the kids who came after them and came before them. Behind the photographs a layer of aluminum foil makes the door look like the entryway to a spaceship.

Open the door and you are inside what Kevin Emerson, the KidLab teacher here, proudly calls "controlled chaos." No wall is bare. Materials are everywhere. The room is criss-crossed by ropes: the sign of a pulley experiment going on in the fourth grade. Behind the pulleys are projects from every grade taped to walls, hanging from the ceiling, sitting on the terrarium. T-shirts with organs painted and labeled on the front hang on a clothesline. A tremendous trash can tangled together with cardboard and duct tape plays the part of an enormous ear canal. Across from the ear canal is a marble roadway under a wooden loft. Sitting next to that, a life-sized wooden skeleton has his femur and fibula appropriately labeled.

"Today," Mr. Emerson tells the students, who are seated on milk crates at a worktable, "we are going to play mini-golf. Who here knows what mini-golf is?"

"It's with clubs and golf balls," Alijah volunteers.

"And what do you do with the club and golf balls?"

"You hit the ball," one student offers.

"You try to get it in the hole," says another.

After he is certain that the students—many of whom have never seen a mini-golf course in their lives—understand the idea, Mr. Emerson moves on. "First, we are going to have to build golf clubs." Mr. Emerson pulls out a club he has built out of a dowel, a Styrofoam head, and a foam handle. "Then we are going to make courses with obstacles and a hole that you have to hit the ball into." As he says this, Mr. Emerson shows the students a sample course he built the day before. "I will give you foam and cardboard. You'll be using glue guns. Does everyone remember how to use the glue guns?"

The class nods.

"Now everyone remember: your golf course needs to be challenging, but not so hard that you can't get a hole-in-one."

And off they go. One by one, they get their dowels and Styrofoam from Mr. Emerson and sit down at one of the three worktables set up in the room. Looking now and then at the sample he has built, they insert their dowel in the Styrofoam and tape on a handle to make their own clubs.

"That looks good," Mr. Emerson says to Jeffrey as he finishes his club. "You can start on your mini-golf course now…"

As students work on their mini-golf courses, Mr. Emerson walks from table to table. Fifteen minutes later, golf courses constructed of blocks of foam and curves of cardboard have sprung up around the KidLab room. The first KidLab period is nearly over. Mr. Emerson tells the class to clean up and ten minutes later they are headed back to Ms. Knight's classroom.

Later in the day, the class returns to KidLab. Mr. Emerson reminds the students of their mini-golf work, but he doesn't need to do much reminding. Soon

At the opening of a lesson, the KidLab teacher ties the classroom activity to a real-world experience.

Every part of the project does not have to tie into a scientific lesson. Here, students start by building golf clubs to get into the lesson.

With questions and suggestions, the KidLab teacher provides students with challenges and support.

Classroom management tools, like Stanley's bowties, are critical to maintaining order within the "controlled chaos" of KidLab.

enough, the third graders are enthusiastically pulling out their mini-golf courses and playing with their putters. Wandering from course to course, Mr. Emerson encourages students to hit their balls and see how they go.

"Why won't the ball go into the hole?" Jeffrey asks in frustration.

Mr. Emerson replies with another question: "What's happening when you do it?"

"It keeps rolling into the corner."

"Then I guess you ought to work on that corner, huh?"

After another fifteen minutes of troubleshooting and problem-solving, Mr. Emerson returns to the front of the classroom. "We've been doing really well today," he says as the students pause from their putting. "I think Stanley's at three bowties." The students turn to see Mr. Emerson raise Stanley's bowtie monitor—a simple piece of construction paper with a Velcro bowtie stuck on—from level two to three. If they are on their best behavior for the rest of the day, they hope to make it to a perfect four.

After fifteen more minutes of playing, Mr. Emerson calls the students to the center of the room, where they take their place on milk crates.

"So, what did everyone observe?" he asks.

Silence at first, then Jeffrey volunteers, "Susan hit the ball real hard once and it went right across the room." The other students laugh.

"Why did it go across the room?"

"'Cause it went off the golf course."

"But how did she hit it?"

"She hit it hard."

"What if she hit it softly?"

"Then it wouldn't have gone so far."

"So, can someone tell me what makes the ball go further?"

"When it bounces off things."

"When you hit it hard."

"When you whack it with the golf club."

"And what makes it not go as far?"

"When you don't whack it with the golf club."

"When you just tap it real lightly."

"That sounds like it happens a lot, doesn't it?" Mr. Emerson says, as he writes this new rule for golf balls on easel pad paper: *When you hit the ball hard, it goes a large distance. When you hit the ball softly, it goes a small distance.*

As the discussion continues, the students make other observations about their courses: which materials cause the ball to bounce and which don't; which way the ball rolls ("Why won't it go uphill? Why did it miss the hole?"). As he hears observations that relate to physics, Mr. Emerson helps steer the conversation into stated rules, compiling these for the students at the front of class.

As this second KidLab period nears its end, Mr. Emerson reads back through the list of rules the students have compiled:

When you hit the ball hard, it goes a large distance. When you hit the ball softly, it goes a small distance.

The ball can't move itself.

The ball only changes direction if it hits something or if the bottom is uneven.

You have to hit the ball harder to make it go uphill than to make it go downhill.

Another day in the life of KidLab is over. On the other hand, judging from the way twenty students in Ms. Knight's class spend the rest of the week chirping about the mini-golf courses they built and the way the ball rolled and why it bounced and what makes it hard to go uphill, the fun of KidLab and the lessons learned there have only just begun.

In post-project reflection, the KidLab teacher helps students connect their observations to scientific principles.

What's the BIG IDEA?

KIDLAB IS HARD TO CATEGORIZE. IT IS SCIENCE *AND* ART. IT IS PROJECT-BASED LEARNING *AND* TRANSMISSION LEARNING. IT IS HANDS-ON, ACTIVITY-DRIVEN, student-centered, experiment-focused, creative, imaginative art-science-play-work-learning-fun.

Below, we'll tell you about some of our theories about what KidLab is… and isn't. But since all of our theories can't quite nail it down, we thought we'd ask the kids. Here's what they had to say:

"The **BEST THING** about KidLab *is* **mESSY** projects."
- Kindergarten Student

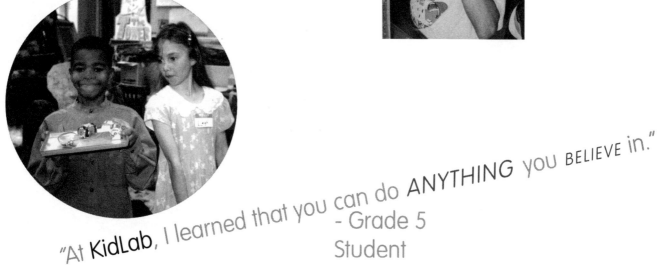

"At KidLab, I learned that you can do ANYTHING you believe in."
- Grade 5 Student

"At KidLab, we learn how to have fun and explore." - Grade 3 Student

"KidLab is kind of like SCIENCE."
- Kindergarten Student

"KidLab is learning, but it's really fun." - Grade 4 Student

It's Project-Based Learning... Right?

In KidLab, student work grows out of a hands-on project. Whether it is building a mini-golf course, a skeleton, or a boat, the students start with little more than a bundle of materials and a question to answer or puzzle to solve. Following their own intuition and inquiries, they see where the project leads them. They hit dead ends and miscues along the way. These mistakes are as valuable as the successes as they learn what works and what does not. Through each step in the project, following their own curiosity, they construct answers to the questions they have been given. This model—student-centered, project-focused, question-based, curiosity-driven—is often called project-based learning.

B U T . . . WE DON'T THINK OF KIDLAB AS JUST PROJECT-BASED LEARNING. Often, KidLab lessons are very focused and hardly as open-ended as most project-based learning. When students build a skeleton, for instance, they are told exactly what they should build, and often given many of the answers. For instance, to create a ball-and-socket joint, students are given a nail, a foam ball, and a cup, and told exactly how to build a mechanism that simulates the joint. At such times, and there are many of them, KidLab is not student-driven and not project-based.

It's Transmission Learning... Right?

In fact, a lot of KidLab is less similar to a project-based model and more similar to a transmission model, in which the teacher explains a concept to students, and the students listen and understand. This model is often used in urban schools that serve underprivileged students who appear to benefit most from highly structured classroom settings. In a lesson on environmental habitats, the KidLab teacher goes over the seven types of habitats with the students, and then the students draw them. The teacher provides the knowledge. The students learn it and show their learning through a structured activity.

B U T . . . WE DON'T THINK OF KIDLAB AS JUST A TRANSMISSION CLASSROOM. After all, there are many lessons in which the KidLab teacher provides very little information at all, and in which students simply follow their intuition and come up with the answers at the end. What both the project-based learning lessons and the transmission lessons have in common is that we involve students in a hands-on exercise that helps them truly see the lesson come to life.

It's Art Class... Right?

Art plays a critical role in KidLab. Students build things and paint things and draw things and put things together. In KidLab, they are carpenters and sculptors and artists. We know that there is more of a chance of remembering a lesson when we are truly engaged in that lesson, and engaged in a variety of ways. KidLab engages students' minds and hands. It appeals to visual learners and kinetic learners, literally drawing students into the lesson. By re-creating what they learn, students are more apt to remember and truly understand lessons.

BUT... WE DON'T THINK OF KIDLAB AS JUST AN ART CLASS. After all, none of the lessons in KidLab are about art. We don't teach about perspective or proportions or shading here. Art is only a tool to unleash creativity and imagination and to involve learners in the process.

It's Science Class... Right?

The KidLab program ties into the science curriculum used in the classroom. In KidLab, students learn not just scientific facts and knowledge, but more importantly scientific thinking, attitudes, and skills. The successful KidLab student learns to think creatively and imaginatively about the human body and the motion of objects and dozens of other things. These ingredients are all part of employing the scientific method and engaging in scientific thinking.

BUT... WE DON'T THINK OF KIDLAB AS JUST A SCIENCE CLASS, because KidLab is as much about hands-on building and art—the kinds of things you'd learn in a carpentry class or an art studio. More than a science class or an art class, KidLab sits at the intersection between science and art.

HOW does KidLab work?

There are six things that happen at KidLab that are critical to the program functioning well.

Mix of Fantasy and Reality

The setup of KidLab brings children into a world that melds art and science, fantasy and reality.

Uncertainty about Answers, Certainty about Support

Through the trial-and-error method, KidLab consistently exposes students to situations in which there is no clear right and wrong answer, but there is clear support for them to explore possible answers.

Follow-through in activities

In KidLab, students engage in extended lessons that progress over time, connecting questions with results.

Hands-on Experience

In KidLab, students have the opportunity to see and touch their work, truly experiencing their lessons and becoming adept with materials.

Model Questions

The KidLab teacher models an inquisitive attitude that pushes students to think through what they are doing and why, and encourages them to ask the same questions themselves.

Use of Diagrams

KidLab puts both student and teacher in the role of explaining what they have learned to others through models, drawings, and discussion.

In the pages that follow, we explore each of these six, looking at them from a number of different angles.

The KidLab Teacher

What skills and attitudes does the KidLab teacher need in order for it to work?

The KidLab Package

What do you need in your KidLab in order for it to work? What are the bare essentials, and what are luxuries? We look at staffing, scheduling, space, and other items, considering how each helps KidLab work.

KidLab: Why it Works

What do students get out of KidLab? How can we tell if KidLab is succeeding? We look at each of four outcomes that come from KidLab: creative thinking, inquisitiveness, academic persistence, and creative doing, and look at how the six things KidLab does help us arrive at the results we want.

KidLab Lessons Plans

Finally, we offer a few tips on how to put together KidLab lessons plans, and offer a few sample lessons plans for you to work with.

KidLab: WHY IT WORKS

KIDLAB IS A PROGRAM NOT SIMPLY IN SCIENTIFIC FACTS AND KNOWLEDGE, BUT MORE IMPORTANTLY IN SCIENTIFIC THINKING, ATTITUDES, AND SKILLS. THE SUCCESSFUL KidLab student does not learn to memorize information about the femur and fibula or force and velocity. Instead, the successful KidLab student learns to think creatively and imaginatively about the human body and the motion of objects and dozens of other things.

The catch phrase in education today, however, is neither *creativity* nor *imagination*. It is *standards*. Those of us who have worked with KidLab recoil when we first hear the word. True, our students have shown significant progress on the state's MCAS science exam, far outstripping students from similar backgrounds and positing higher scores each year the test has been administered. But *standards*, to us, sounds like the antithesis of what KidLab is about. *Standards* sounds like it means facts and figures, everyone doing the same thing and parroting back the same knowledge.

But, in fact, *standards* does not have to mean that at all. Standards, instead, can simply mean: being clear about what you want to get out of a day, and defining the markers that tell you whether you've gotten there. At KidLab, we want to get creative thinking, inquisitiveness, academic persistence and creative doing.

AT KIDLAB, WE HAVE DEVELOPED **STANDARDS** FOR THE **SKILLS AND ATTITUDES** WE EXPECT KIDS TO DEVELOP, BASING THESE ON THE MASSACHUSETTS FRAMEWORKS.

creative thinking

inquisitiveness

academic persistence

creative doing

We have developed standards to measure each of these, aligning them with the Massachusetts frameworks for science and technology. With these standards, over time we can say: KidLab makes a difference in ways that a pencil-and-paper test will never show.

CREATIVE creative THINKING
creative

Good creative thinkers have one foot in fantasy and one foot in reality. In the world of fantasy, they can imagine what might be, pose tantalizing questions that lead in a thousand directions. This must, however, be grounded in the world of reality, where they test how the things they imagine apply to their actual experience. Students who can successfully thrive in these two worlds are poised to be creative thinkers, scientists, and artists.

In order to measure creative thinking, we have divided it into three parts—imagination, open mindedness, and critical reasoning—and set standards of excellence in each:

Imagination
Children who excel at using their imaginations are...

❶ willing and able to picture themselves in a fictitious situation.

They will ❷ accept the parameters that are given in describing that situation...

...and are able to ❸ logically apply those to the game or puzzle they face.

They are then able to ❹ use this fictitious situation to arrive at conclusions and solutions.

"Advances in science and technology depend on our staying open to new ideas and then examining them with a critical eye... To attain rigor in these disciplines, students must learn to suspend disbelief, entertain new ideas, and be wary of information not supported by good evidence. They must also recognize that all theories remain ever open to reconsideration."
-Massachusetts Frameworks

Open Mindedness
Open-minded students are...

❶ willing to accept when they are wrong...

...and ❷ recognize that every answer is not black-and-white.

They ❸ listen to explanations from others...

...and ❹ use these to adjust their own theories of how the world works and what is right and wrong.

Critical Reasoning
When facing a new situation, someone with good critical reasoning skills will...

❶ apply prior knowledge...

...and use it to ❷ make judgments about the situation.

He or she can ❸ prove or disprove previously unencountered points based on past experience.

WHAT does **KidLab** do?

We have designed KidLab so that it will help kids develop their creative thinking skills as well as help those who have developed these skills to shine in ways that they may not in a traditional classroom. There are three key ways that KidLab does this (outlined on page 18):

Mix of Fantasy and Reality
The setup of KidLab brings children into a world that melds art and science, fantasy and reality. By tying real experiments to fanciful ideas, children are encouraged to use their imagination without ever losing sight of the real-life results of what they are doing.

Uncertainty about Answers, Certainty about Support
By presenting hands-on experiments to children in an open-ended way, KidLab also exposes children to situations where there is no clear right and wrong answer. Few mini-golf courses work exactly as the children had imagined they would, and few boats sail in exactly the direction they hoped. But each improvement and test of that mini-golf course or boat helps them get closer to their goals or discover an error in their ways.

Hands-on Experience
The opportunity to see and touch their work is particularly appealing for many students who might not do well in the more antiseptic world of traditional classroom learning. Students who are adept at applying past ideas to present situations will be more successful in KidLab than they might elsewhere and have the opportunity to shine by showing that they can bridge concepts.

KidLab puts kids on the path to creative thinking. Start with a student who appears unimaginative and close-minded, and has difficulties with critical thinking. Put that student through the Amazing KidLab-izer and you help build the qualities of imagination, open mindedness, and critical thinking!

BEFORE...

Unimaginative

- Cannot translate elements of story into practice.

- Unwilling to "play along" with fiction.

MIX OF FANTASY AND REALITY

Experimental method and artistic approach consistently exposes students to fictitious situations with tangible manifestation.

Close-minded

- Emotionally hurt by being wrong.

- Argues persistently and won't accept own ability and skill level. Defensive and defiant.

- Will insist on being right even in the face of conflicting evidence. Does not budge from preconceived notions of what is right.

UNCERTAINTY ABOUT ANSWERS, CERTAINTY ABOUT SUPPORT

Consistently exposes students to uncertainty in which there is no clear right and wrong, but there is clear support for work and for pursuing scientific conclusions.

Poor Critical Reasoning

- Takes consistently simplistic approach without connecting to prior work.

- Questions outside assistance with skepticism: "What are you talking about?"

HANDS-ON EXPERIENCE

Appeals to students who may have difficulty with traditional classroom learning styles. Makes it easier for these students to communicate and apply knowledge learned experientially.

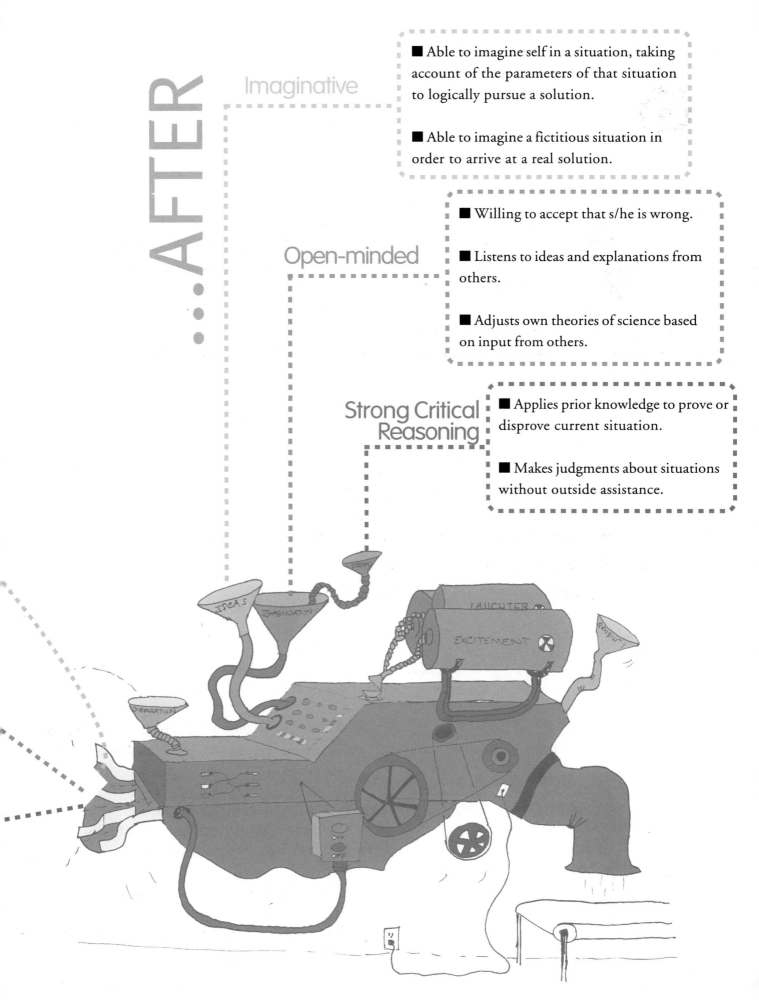

AFTER...

Imaginative

■ Able to imagine self in a situation, taking account of the parameters of that situation to logically pursue a solution.

■ Able to imagine a fictitious situation in order to arrive at a real solution.

Open-minded

■ Willing to accept that s/he is wrong.

■ Listens to ideas and explanations from others.

■ Adjusts own theories of science based on input from others.

Strong Critical Reasoning

■ Applies prior knowledge to prove or disprove current situation.

■ Makes judgments about situations without outside assistance.

inquisitiveness

Without a doubt, every child has an inborn curiosity and inquisitive nature. Children continually want to know more. The challenge of good teaching is to help them seize upon that inquisitiveness and turn it towards gaining valuable skills and knowledge.

In order to measure inquisitiveness, we have divided it into two parts— scientific curiosity and focus—and set standards of excellence in each:

Scientific Curiosity
Children who exhibit "scientific curiosity" will...

❶ ask questions about how and why the world works the way it does.

They will also ❷ independently seek answers to their questions...

❸ thinking through where and how they can learn more.

Focus
Well-focused children will...

❶ keep their attention on a single question or idea long enough to investigate and explore it, following up on relevant ideas.

These children will also see the continuity and connection between various experiences. This will show up in the fact that they ❷ ask questions relevant to lessons...

❸ try lessons from the classroom at home...

...and ❹ volunteer comparisons between lessons and other experiences.

"At the heart of science and technology is the invitation to pursue questions about our world. Children meet these questions with an innate curiosity that effective teaching can bend gently toward science. Sometimes curiosity resembles puzzlement or confusion. Other times it resembles fascination, amazement, looking closer, revising ideas, and persistence. Curiosity in all its forms needs to be encouraged and kept alive in our students if they are to embrace science and technology."
-Massachusetts Frameworks

We have designed KidLab to foster students' scientific curiosity and focus. This occurs in two ways (outlined on page 18):

Model Questions

The first thing that motivates students to raise questions about KidLab lessons is having a teacher who does exactly that. By bringing his own inquisitiveness and asking his own questions about how the world works, the KidLab teacher models the behavior that is expected of children. This, in turn, pushes children to ask questions.

OPEN-ENDED INQUIRIES

The questions that are posed to students are not always easily answered. Sometimes they are left open in discussion with answers coming only out of the experience of building and testing ideas. This allows children to follow their curiosity with a goal in mind.

Follow-through in Activities

KidLab encourages students to be focused by setting up experiments and activities that simply cannot be completed or figured out in a short time. In order for children to follow from the questions that preceded their experiment to the reflection that follows it, they must maintain focus and attention.

KidLab puts kids on the path to inquisitiveness. Start with a student who appears scientifically bored and unfocused. Put that student through the Amazing KidLab-izer and you help build the qualities of scientific curiosity and focus.

BEFORE...

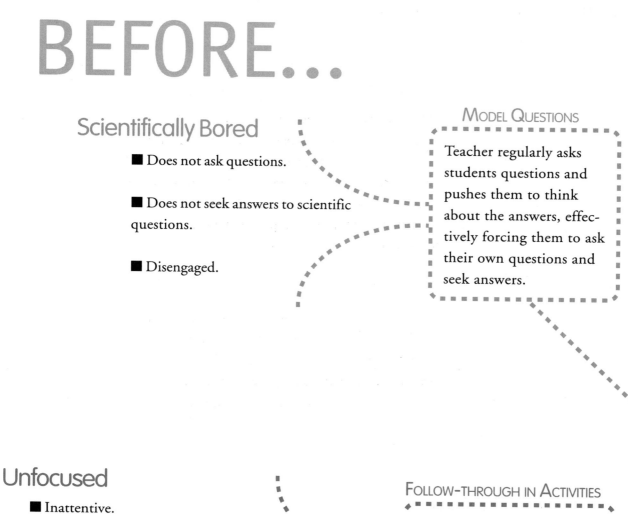

Scientifically Bored

- Does not ask questions.

- Does not seek answers to scientific questions.

- Disengaged.

MODEL QUESTIONS

Teacher regularly asks students questions and pushes them to think about the answers, effectively forcing them to ask their own questions and seek answers.

Unfocused

- Inattentive.

- Does not get engaged in experimenting; does not work hard.

- Does not connect ideas within lesson.

FOLLOW-THROUGH IN ACTIVITIES

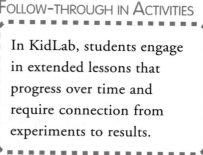

In KidLab, students engage in extended lessons that progress over time and require connection from experiments to results.

...AFTER

Scientifically Curious

- Raises questions related to science lesson.

- Independently seeks answers to questions.

- Asks "Why?" not just "How?"

Focused

- Maintains attention on a question long enough to investigate and explore it.

- Tries lessons from classroom at home.

- Volunteers comparisons between lesson and other experiences.

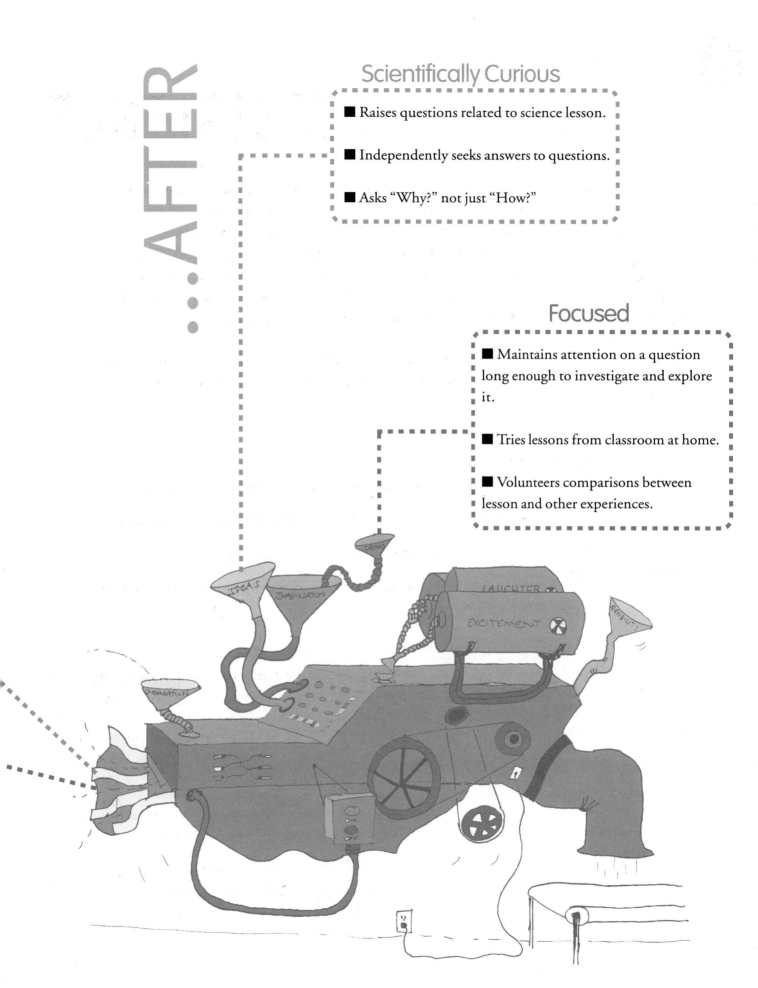

ACADEMIC
academic
academic PERSISTENCE

Too often in school settings, children are given assignments where they know the challenge is to find the "right" answer. If they succeed, they do well. If they do not, they have failed and try to learn the right answer so that they will succeed next time. The real world is hardly as clean. To succeed, we need to be able to confront the same challenges over and over again and turn failures into successes. We need the confidence to take on challenges, but also the resilience to continue taking them on when they seem insurmountable.

In order to measure academic persistence, we have divided it into two parts—confidence and strategy in taking risks—and set standards of excellence in each:

Confidence

Confidence shows in a child's...

❶ willingness to admit uncertainty and doubt by asking questions...

...or ❷ venturing possible answers, without worrying about "looking stupid."

Confident children will be ❸ willing to stop and start over when they need to overcome a challenge...

...and will ❹ move ahead after making mistakes and use those mistakes to inform what they do in the future.

Strategy in Taking Risks

Confidence should be balanced with a strategic approach to taking risks. Children who have this strategic approach will...

❶ follow up initial questions with further probing on a topic, not letting a challenge frustrate them.

They will have the ability to ❷ come up with new methods and approaches to a problem and will independently test these out.

They will ❸ consider different scenarios in approaching a problem, posing hypotheses about what would happen if they pursued these scenarios.

"A tolerance for complexity and ambiguity helps students persist in the face of messy data or procedural uncertainties. Willingness to risk failure, to begin again, to find a new strategy, or to fine-tune an existing one helps us to come up with better explanations and solutions in all areas of science and technology."
-Massachusetts Frameworks

We have designed KidLab to build students' confidence in an environment where it pays to be persistent and strategic in taking risks. This is supported in three ways (outlined on page 18):

Uncertainty about Answers, Certainty About Support

The activities and experiments that kids conduct in KidLab consistently expose them to situations in which the outcome and conclusions are unclear. As students become accustomed to this, they recognize that there will not often be a clear right and wrong answer but that they will have the support of the teacher in pursuing their hypotheses about possible answers and seeing where they lead.

Follow-through in Activities

Since students don't know what the outcome of their activities will be, they often must test ideas and hypotheses by trial and error. While successes thankfully occur, more often a trial is not completely successful. Students are thus forced to face failure regularly and to consider how to move beyond it and use it to meet with success.

Model Questions

In order to encourage strategic thinking about risk-taking, the KidLab teacher will pose questions to students as they are working, forcing them in the process to think through what they are doing and why. This provides students with an opportunity to see mistakes and address them. While the teacher will provide support, students are left to themselves to decide how to use it.

KidLab puts kids on the path to academic persistence. Start with a student who appears overly timid and insecure. Put that student through the Amazing KidLab-izer and you help build the qualities of confidence and strategy in taking risks!

BEFORE...

Overly Timid

■ Gives up in frustration after one challenge.

■ Immediately asks someone else to do it for them before trying it themselves.

■ Tries to sabotage project or give up when it is not working.

MODEL QUESTIONS

Teacher poses questions to students as they are working, providing opportunity to see mistakes and address them. Support is provided, but students are left to themselves to decide how to use it.

Insecure Student

■ Afraid to restate ideas, not wanting to look stupid. "Forget about it," when asked.

UNCERTAINTY ABOUT ANSWERS, CERTAINTY ABOUT SUPPORT

Consistently exposes students to uncertainty in which there is no clear right and wrong, but there is clear support for work and for pursuing scientific conclusions.

Insecure Student

■ Gives up, saying "I don't care... This is stupid... I can't."

■ Doesn't show pride in work.

FOLLOW-THROUGH IN ACTIVITIES

Trial and error approach forces students to confront failure regularly and try various methods. Frustration will become an obstacle to learning otherwise.

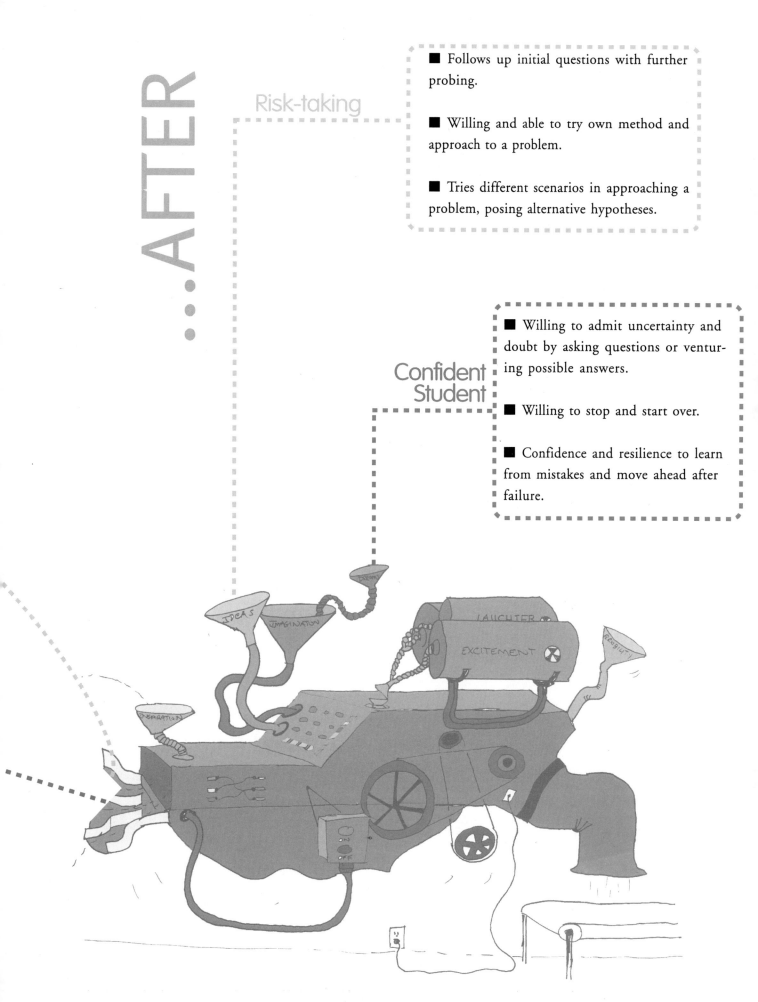

...AFTER

Risk-taking

■ Follows up initial questions with further probing.

■ Willing and able to try own method and approach to a problem.

■ Tries different scenarios in approaching a problem, posing alternative hypotheses.

Confident Student

■ Willing to admit uncertainty and doubt by asking questions or venturing possible answers.

■ Willing to stop and start over.

■ Confidence and resilience to learn from mistakes and move ahead after failure.

GOAL ⊙ CREATIVE creative DOING creative creative

As important as creative thinking (see pages 22-25) may be, it is only the tip of the iceberg. We want students who are creative *doers*. These are students who know how to use tools and materials to turn their imaginative ideas into three-dimensional reality. A creative doer can describe how things work and figure out how to fix them when they don't. A creative doer is adept with technology—not technology in the new sense of clicking a mouse and typing at a keyboard, but technology in the old sense of building structures, putting things together, taking things apart, and understanding how it all works.

In order to measure creative doing, we have divided it into two parts—comfort with materials and effectiveness at design—and set standards of excellence in each:

Comfort with Materials
Children who are comfortable with materials are able to...

❶ approach a mechanical problem by offering ideas of materials that they would use...

...and proceed to ❷ use materials available to construct a mechanism to help solve the problem.

In doing so, students ❸ use materials safely as well.

"During the elementary school years, students' experiences with technology are hands-on and exploratory; they encounter technology issues long before they know what technology is... But while most students in grades Pre-K through four are fascinated with technology, they need to experience the mechanisms, principles, and design constraints that underlie technological solutions."
-Massachusetts Frameworks

Effective with Design
Good designers can...

❶ create accurate diagrams that represent what they want to build or what others have built.

In doing so they are able to ❷ communicate and demonstrate design so that others can do the same.

We have designed KidLab to help students become progressively more comfortable with materials and more effective at explaining and representing designs. This is supported in two ways (outlined on page 18):

Hands-on Experience

The activities and experiments that kids conduct in KidLab consistently expose them to a variety of tools, materials, and hands-on use of both. Students who are not comfortable with materials initially gain that comfort through their work in KidLab.

Use of Diagrams

As students work on their projects using the materials available, they often must take ideas presented by the KidLab teacher and translate those ideas into hands-on reality. By modeling the use of diagrams and helping students to turn those diagrams into hands-on projects, the KidLab teacher models and teaches effective design.

KidLab puts kids on the path to creative doing. Start with a student who appears uncomfortable with materials and ineffective in design. Put that student through the Amazing KidLab-izer and you help build the qualities of comfort with materials and efficacy in design!

BEFORE...

Uncomfortable with Materials

- Uncomfortable with tools and materials.

- Cannot think of materials to use to address a particular problem.

- Unable to suggest ways of combining materials to create new structures or devices.

HANDS-ON EXPERIENCE

Hands-on lessons regularly expose students to use of tools and materials, while open-ended approach forces kids to discover new and creative ways of employing materials.

Ineffective Designer

- Has difficulty drawing diagrams that accurately represent a subject.

- Does not have clear sense of how to use proportion and symbols for diagrams.

- Cannot communicate design concepts.

USE OF DIAGRAMS

KidLab teacher uses diagrams to illustrate lessons and engages students in activities that put them in the role of explaining and showing to others what they have done.

...AFTER

Comfortable with Materials

■ Comfortable with using a variety of materials safely and effectively.

■ Approaches a mechanical problem by thinking about and suggesting materials to use.

■ Adept at using a variety of objects together to construct something new.

Effective Designer

■ Can create accurate diagrams.

■ Uses symbols and representation to develop useful diagrams.

■ Is able to communicate and demonstrate design so that others can do the same.

THE KidLab Package:

from basic...

	YUGO OF KIDLABS (THE BARE MINIMUM)	TOYOTA OF KIDLABS (WHAT WE HAVE)	MERCEDES OF KIDLABS (THE DELUXE MODEL)
Staffing			
KIDLAB STAFF	Part-time specialist	Full-time specialist	Full-time specialist and assistant
STUDENTS PER ADULT	18-25	10-18	Less than 10
Schedule			
TIME BLOCKS	Two 45-minute class periods	Less than three hours	Three to four hours
CLASSROOM TIE-IN	KidLab planned to fit with school science curriculum	Coordinated planning of classroom science and KidLab	Weekly meetings with classroom teacher
FOLLOW-UP TIME	None	None	One class period

SEE FOLLOWING PAGES
FOR EXPLANATION...

Space

	YUGO OF KIDLABS (THE BARE MINIMUM)	TOYOTA OF KIDLABS (WHAT WE HAVE)	MERCEDES OF KIDLABS (THE DELUXE MODEL)
LEARNING CENTERS	One work center for every 8-10 students	One work center for every 6-8 students	One work center for every 4-6 students
STORAGE SPACE	About 20-30 square feet	About 30-50 square feet	About 50-100 square feet
DISPLAY SPACE	Limited space in KidLab, but projects displayed around school	Tape it, hang it, string it, just show it!	A whole lotta display in and out of KidLab

Stuff

BEHAVIOR MANAGEMENT TOOLS	Ritual games that fit in with KidLab and provide behavioral expectations	Ritual games that fit in with KidLab and provide behavioral expectations	Ritual games that fit in with KidLab and provide behavioral expectations
CURIOSITY SPARKERS	Photograhps, old projects	Photographs, old projects, plants, shelves for ongoing experiments	Photographs, old projects, plants, aquarium, shelves for ongoing experiments, some animals
WATER	Easily accessible	Easily accessible	Sink in KidLab
TOOLS AND MATERIALS	Enough space for tools and materials for the next set of lessons	Materials with clear method for cleanup	Workbench and closet for materials
SUPER DOHKA DOHKA	Super Dohka Dohka board the size of a board game	Super Dohka Dohka board the size of a wall	Super Dohka Dohka board the size of Texas

...to deluxe

KidLab Staffing

KidLab Staff

KidLab requires a science specialist who has time to devote to the program. While there are ideas from KidLab that can be taken and adapted to an individual classroom, we recommend that if your school is truly going to reap the benefits of KidLab, it have a specialist who can devote some time and thought every week to making KidLab work.

Students per Adult

One of the key components for a successful KidLab is a low student-to-adult ratio. If you can set up your KidLab with less than ten students for every adult, you are doing very well. These adults do not need to be teachers—paraprofessionals, college interns, or parent volunteers could be other good KidLab supervisors. More than twenty to twenty-five students in a KidLab is not recommended, as the amount of materials and tools needed become unmanageable.

AT NEIGHBORHOOD HOUSE, WE REDUCE THE NUMBER OF STUDENTS BY SPLITTING CLASSES INTO SMALL GROUPS THAT ROTATE BETWEEN KIDLAB AND THEIR REGULAR CLASSROOM. THIS PROVIDES TEACHERS WITH PLANNING TIME AND MAKES THE STUDENT BODY MANAGEABLE IN THE CHAOS OF KIDLAB.

Time Blocks

KidLab requires a process of investigation, experimentation, and follow-up observation. This takes time, and it is only with difficulty that KidLab can fit into a traditional 45-minute class schedule. Ideally, KidLab provides sufficient time for students to go through every step of the process—about three hours.

AT NEIGHBORHOOD HOUSE, WE HAVE KIDLAB DAYS FOR ONE CLASS ONCE EVERY TWO WEEKS. THIS SETUP ALLOWS US TO APPORTION A LARGE TIME BLOCK TO KIDLAB IN A WAY THAT TEACHERS AND STUDENTS ARE PREPARED FOR. TEACHERS BENEFIT WITH ADDITIONAL PLANNING TIME, WHILE STUDENTS TEND TO LOOK FORWARD TO THEIR BI-WEEKLY EXCURSION INTO THE LAB.

Classroom Tie-In

At its best, KidLab is carefully connected into the school's curriculum, with experiments and activities in KidLab complementing science lessons in the classroom. Classroom teachers meet regularly with the KidLab teacher to plan science lessons together. In less than ideal circumstances, the KidLab teacher might design lessons to fit in with the overall science curriculum, but with minimal communication with classroom teachers.

AT NEIGHBORHOOD HOUSE, THE KIDLAB TEACHER "FRONTLOADS" MEETINGS WITH NEW CLASSROOM TEACHERS, PLANNING TOGETHER EVERY WEEK TO FIRST DEVELOP AN APPROPRIATELY CONNECTED CURRICULUM, THEN TAPERING MEETINGS OFF AS A RHYTHM IS ESTABLISHED.

Follow-Up Time

At its best, KidLab would include follow-up time after students have completed an experiment and had time to think about it, when the KidLab teacher can take a half-hour to an hour to return to the idea and give students the opportunity to test the theories they came up with.

KidLab Space

Learning Centers

For the hands-on, experiential learning that happens in KidLab, it is best to have the room divided into small learning centers where groups of up to six students can engage in a similar project. Appropriate objects and visual devices can be used to differentiate space and provide places to build as well as other places to test experiments.

> AT NEIGHBORHOOD HOUSE, WE HAVE AUGMENTED OUR THREE WORK CENTERS WITH SKYLAB: A MAKESHIFT LOFT THAT STUDENTS CAN USE TO TEST EXPERIMENTS RANGING FROM THE SPEED OF FALLING OBJECTS TO THE ELASTICITY OF SILLY PUTTY.

Storage Space

Any KidLab will require a variety of materials and tools that must be stored from lesson to lesson. At Neighborhood House, we have a storage closet and corners of the room reserved for materials, totaling about 30-50 square feet of space.

Display Space

Part of the *ah-ha!* of KidLab is that students see the work of their peers and the many ways that others addressed the same challenge. Having at least some display space is therefore critical to KidLab. Projects can be taped to walls, hung from ceilings, or strung across rooms, as long as they are seen and seen prominently.

Behavior Management Tools

In the chaos of KidLab, it helps to have some established tools to ground children and establish behavioral expectations. These can take any form, but we recommend making sure that you have them and that they fit in with the feeling of your KidLab.

> At Neighborhood House, we have developed three behavior management rituals for the class. Stanley's Bowties serve as a group behavior monitor; the Raceway allows students to gauge progress; Clean Up Badges distribute responsibility for clean-up.

Curiosity Sparkers

When kids enter KidLab, you want them to enter a world where everything sparks their curiosity and their imagination. Little things strategically placed around the KidLab space can help to achieve this. Animals are a good touch—an aquarium, a terrarium, though not too many. A growing space for plants adds to the interest. It also helps to have a space for ongoing experiments and old projects to sit or hang or otherwise make themselves known.

> At Neighborhood House, we have a pet lizard and (occasionally) fish. A third terrarium stores an old pumpkin that is the subject of a yearlong experiment.

Water

Two parts hydrogen, one part oxygen. Who would think something so simple could be so useful? But, as any science teacher knows, it is ultra-useful: for experiments, for clean-up, for washing hands.

Tools and Materials

We use wood and foam and rubber bands and plastic cup lids. We use hammers and glue guns and saws and scissors. We have marble roadways and candle wax and old egg cartons. The important thing is that *we never stop acquiring materials*: Packets of sugar and take-out trays should never be thrown out. That cheap trash can that you used for a lesson on sound waves can be re-used for a lesson on ear canals. Ideally, you'd have a workbench and closet to store all these things. At a minimum, you should have an ordered system for children to put them back in their appropriate places.

And of course...

Super Dokha Dokha

No KidLab would be complete without Super Dokha Dokha. (Actually, any KidLab would be complete without Super Dokha Dokha, but it's too much fun to leave out of our description.) A grid of nails in a wooden board—it's reminiscent of Plinko from *The Price Is Right*, and provides for a fun game and a math and science lesson all in one. Every now and then, if the kids have acted on their best behavior and the KidLab teacher feels they deserve it, they get to each take a few tosses at the Super Dokha Dokha board. If their ping pong ball lands in the board, it tumbles down the nails, following a random path. Each class keeps track of where the ball ends up at the bottom, with the pattern expected to approximate a bell curve over time. In virtually every grade, we found kids who think of Super Dokha Dokha as the main draw of KidLab.

When children enter KidLab they feel as if they are in a different world. Perhaps the most important part of creating this different world isn't the space where KidLab takes place, but rather the person who makes it happen. When you become a KidLab teacher, you must take on the persona of KidLab: patient and persistent, creative and curious, imaginative and a little eccentric. Some of these are things that you must look for when hiring the teacher, but some are things that Mr. Emerson—the KidLab teacher here—has "grown into" as he has learned to fit into the KidLab world.

THREE CRITICAL KIDLAB SKILLS

If we were to boil the KidLab teacher's job down to one sentence, it would be this: *to create situations in which children can express themselves through science.* In order to do this, there are three things that teachers simply *must* have:

STRONG VISUAL SKILLS AND CREATIVITY

ACTIVE INTEREST AND INVOLVEMENT IN SCIENCE

A GREAT DEAL OF PATIENCE

the KidLab TEACHER

three
KidLab
MUSTS

Active interest and involvement in science

At first glance, KidLab might not appear to need the same high level of science background as, for instance, a chemistry laboratory with its Bunsen burners and chemical hoods. Yet it is for exactly this reason that a strong understanding of science is in fact the single most critical quality for the KidLab teacher. In a chemistry lab, a teacher can rely on materials to guide the experiment. In KidLab, the teacher must make these connections without the aid of materials that "look" scientific.

To inspire children's curiosity to see science in the mundane, the KidLab teacher must first have that same curiosity. The first criterion for any KidLab teacher is that he or she have a strong grounding in science, confidence in that scientific ability, and easy access to good science resources, such as college textbooks.

The kids notice this not only in what the KidLab teacher explains to them, but in how he or she participates. Several kids note that Mr. Emerson does experiments, just like they do, that he not only answers their questions, but "figures things out by himself," too. In this sense, Mr. Emerson models curiosity by being scientifically aware of everything from the plastic cups that can be recycled into ball-and-socket joints to the lizard in the KidLab terrarium.

Strong visual skills and creativity

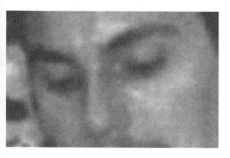

KidLab is, in part, a student-centered classroom where children explore and follow their imagination. But it is also, in part, a teacher-directed environment where students get clear explanations that give them a firm foundation on which to explore. Students are quick to point out that Mr. E "explains things in simple ways" and "shows us what we're going to be doing" before it happens. A good KidLab teacher will be able to combine explanations and visual aids, modeling experiments and commanding enough artistic ability to sketch quick drawings.

Patience

KidLab is, by design, a chaotic place. The KidLab teacher must be able to balance this chaos with an enormous dose of patience. As kids handle glue guns and two-by-fours and run from marble roadways to hot wax, the KidLab teacher must be confident in their ability to handle difficult situations and patient with their progress in an unpredictable atmosphere.

We have also identified a variety of other "pluses" that it helps for a KidLab teacher to have. Many of these are skills that we would expect any classroom teacher to have, and some are unique to KidLab. None are as critical as the three "musts".

Thriftiness and creativity

Teaching what it is, all teachers need to be able to be creative in how they stretch a dollar to cover a variety of lessons. KidLab is no exception. By turning trashcans into enormous ear canals and paper cups into ball-and-socket joints, the KidLab teacher takes this skill to new heights. As long as the teacher has a strong command of scientific ideas, however, the ideas for materials can come more naturally. For some possible sources of materials, see the next page.

YES, THAT'S A CABBAGE. BUT AT KIDLAB, EVEN LEAFY GREENS SERVE THEIR PURPOSE: HERE, THE KIDLAB TEACHER LEADS THE CLASS IN MAKING LITMUS PAPER.

Range

Since we recommend that schools have a dedicated KidLab teacher, that teacher likely has to work with a wide range of ages. This skill is a particular challenge in science, where explanations for a five-year-old can be very different from those for a ten-year-old.

Eccentricity

"The best thing about KidLab is Mr. E," one student tells us, "because he is funny and he is just cool." Many students talk about how "funny" and "goofy" Mr. Emerson is in everything he does from walking to drinking coffee. This is not absolutely necessary, but does help produce the fun and otherworldly feel of KidLab.

10 STEPS TO CREATE YOUR OWN
KidLab Projects

1. Look at the Massachusetts science frameworks and school science curriculum for topics.

2. Flip through "hands on" science books for project ideas.

3. Look through college textbooks for drawings and diagrams that might spark ideas.

4. Use the Massachusetts inquiry and technology standards to design the project's steps and discussion.

5. Think about the levels of ability and independence of your students and tailor your project to warrant an appropriate amount of skill, scientific knowledge, and depth of discussion.

6. Find necessary materials from a variety of places: students' homes, other teachers, recycling centers, Home Depot, local businesses, nearby parks or ponds, arts and crafts stores, etc.

7. Try the project yourself to troubleshoot problem areas.

8. While students are working allow them to take ownership of their projects, and guide them while they take projects in new directions.

9. When carrying out experiential learning projects be an active learner yourself and always look for better ways to complete projects.

10. Take the time to write down what went well and what did not go as well so that the following year you can improve the lesson.

Most KidLab projects have one or more of the following three aspects:

Experimenting

Projects in which students form a hypothesis and test it. (For example, see *Erosion, Boat Building, Mini Golf.*)

Modeling

Projects in which students create a model to represent something that is harder to see or touch in real life. (For example, see lesson plans on *Cells, The Little Things, The Human Body, The Earth and Its Properties.*)

Experiencing

Projects in which students re-create an experience in order to better remember a lesson. (For example, see *Natural Disaster, Erosion, Mini Golf.*)

Science Standards

By its nature, every KidLab lesson addresses a large number of the elementary and middle school standards in the Massachusetts Science & Technology Frameworks Strand 1 (Inquiry) and Strand 3 (Technology). The state standards in these strands are captured in the KidLab standards of Inquisitiveness and Creative Doing, discussed earlier in this book.

The pages that follow provide plans for a handful of KidLab lessons. Each lesson can take from a few minutes to a few hours to set up. To help you gauge the amount of time involved beforehand, we've tried to gauge how much preparation each lesson requires. All but one of the lessons listed requires a low or medium amount of preparation. We included one lesson (Natural Disaster) that requires a high level of preparation in order to give you a taste of the amount of work that goes into it.

	Domain of Science	Level of Preparation
Pangaea Pete Flipbooks	Life	L
Boat Building	Physical	M
Cells	Life	M
The Earth and its Properties	Earth	L
Erosion	Earth	M
The Little Things	Physical	L
Looking Inside the Human Body	Life	L
Mini-Golf	Physical	M
Natural Disaster	Earth	H

Experimenting with . . .

DOMAIN OF SCIENCE: Physical Science (and others)
COMPLEXITY OF PREPARATION: Low   Medium   High

Every kid has heard their science teacher tell them that "science is all around you." The *Experimenting With…* activities prove it by having students engage in experiments with all sorts of household items. *Experimenting with…* projects promote inquiry and familiarize students with the process of developing their own experiments and using the scientific method.

GOAL: DESIGN AND CONDUCT AN EXPERIMENT USING SCIENTIFIC METHOD.

Objectives:

■ Develop creative experiments using everyday items
■ Gain an understanding of the scientific method of posing and testing hypotheses
■ Record data based on experimental observations
■ Accept or reject a hypothesis based on experimentation

Estimated Time Line

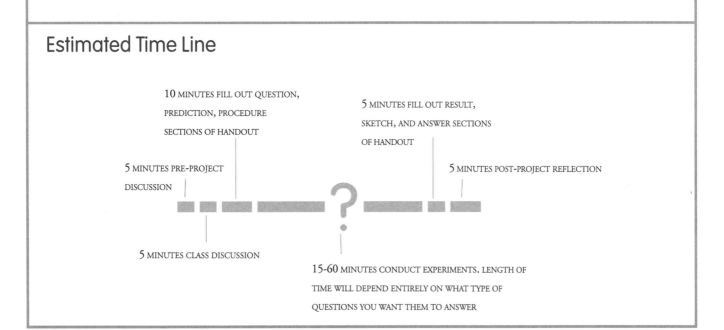

10 MINUTES FILL OUT QUESTION, PREDICTION, PROCEDURE SECTIONS OF HANDOUT

5 MINUTES FILL OUT RESULT, SKETCH, AND ANSWER SECTIONS OF HANDOUT

5 MINUTES PRE-PROJECT DISCUSSION

5 MINUTES POST-PROJECT REFLECTION

5 MINUTES CLASS DISCUSSION

15-60 MINUTES CONDUCT EXPERIMENTS. LENGTH OF TIME WILL DEPEND ENTIRELY ON WHAT TYPE OF QUESTIONS YOU WANT THEM TO ANSWER

Preparation

Choose a subject for the *Experimenting With...* project. Food is often a good bet. Examples include:

- ☐ Candy
- ☐ Snow
- ☐ Silly putty
- ☐ Gummy worms
- ☐ Cereal
- ☐ Marshmallows

The possibilities are truly endless!

Pre-Project Discussion

Show and discuss the item you will be experimenting with (for example, Silly putty). If this is the first time you are doing *Experimenting With...*, introduce the Design-Your-Own-Experiment Sheet.

Proecdure

1. As a class, discuss potential questions to be studied (For example, How long will it stretch before it breaks? Does it stick differently to carpet, wood, painted wood, paper? How will it react to other substances like vinegar, baking soda, and water?)
2. Have students fill out the **question**, **prediction**, and **procedure** parts of the *Design your own experiment* sheet.
3. Check student's sheets for potential trouble spots.
4. Students conduct appropriate experiments
5. Students fill out the **result**, **sketch**, and **answer** sections of their *Design your own experiment* sheet.

Post Project Reflection

What did you observe?

Have some students share their experiments with the class and discuss what questions they might want to study next time.

Trouble Spots

■ The formulation of answerable questions can be tricky. Students sometimes get carried away and want to undertake experiments that are too outrageous or even dangerous. (e.g., I want to see what happens when you throw it out the window.)

■ Sometimes questions for experimentation are not challenging enough.

■ Timing the experiments so that they all take about the same amount of time can also be tricky.

Variations & Extensions

■ Use a Know, Want to know, Learned (KWL) chart to map students' ideas in each of these categories

■ After students finish their experiments, have them pose a new question that takes their results further

Design your own Experiment!

MY QUESTION IS: _____

_____

I PREDICT THAT: _____

_____

PROCEDURE - HERE'S HOW I WILL FIND THE ANSWER TO MY QUESTION:

1._____

2._____

3._____

4._____

5._____

6._____

RESULT - THIS IS WHAT REALLY HAPPENED: _____

_____

_____

HERE'S A SKETCH OF WHAT I DID:

THE ANSWER TO MY QUESTION IS: _____

_____

Pangaea Pete Flipbooks

DOMAIN OF SCIENCE:	Physical Science	**Life Science**	Earth Science
COMPLEXITY OF PREPARATION:	**Low**	Medium	High

Children are fascinated by fairy tale animals and fantastic creatures. Animal Adaptation Flipbooks give them the opportunity to make their own creatures, coupled with the challenge of making those creatures scientifically adaptable to the environment. In the process, they learn about earth habitats and consider concepts underlying evolution.

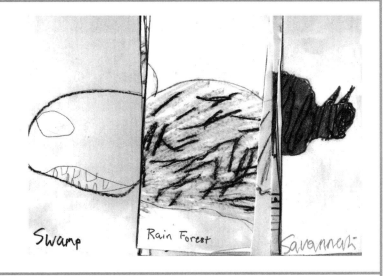

Swamp   Rain Forest   Savannah

Objectives:

GOAL: USE AN ANIMAL FLIPBOOK TO ILLUSTRATE AND EXPLAIN HOW CLIMATE AFFECTS ADAPTATION OF SPECIES

- Gain familiarity with concepts of the seven earth habitats
- Invent animals that have the necessary characteristics to survive in different climate regions
- Develop sketches and drawings of invented animals with adaptive features
- Explain purposes behind invented adaptations

Estimated Time Line with Suggested Stopping Points

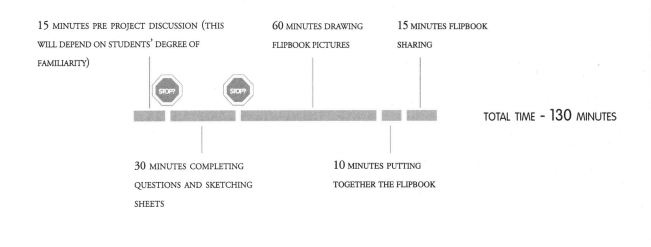

15 MINUTES PRE PROJECT DISCUSSION (THIS WILL DEPEND ON STUDENTS' DEGREE OF FAMILIARITY)

60 MINUTES DRAWING FLIPBOOK PICTURES

15 MINUTES FLIPBOOK SHARING

30 MINUTES COMPLETING QUESTIONS AND SKETCHING SHEETS

10 MINUTES PUTTING TOGETHER THE FLIPBOOK

TOTAL TIME - 130 MINUTES

Applicable Standards from the Massachusetts Science & Technology Frameworks

By its nature, every KidLab lesson addresses almost all of the elementary and middle school standards in Strand 1 (Inquiry) and Strand 3 (Technology) of the Science & Technology Frameworks. In addition, this lesson addresses the following standards in Strand 2 (Domains of Science, Life Sciences):

■ Characteristics of Organisms
>   ■ Observe and describe that animals and plants have different structures which serve different functions in growth, survival, and reproduction. These contribute to the well-being of the whole organism, and to the success of its off-spring.

■ Diversity and Adaptation of Organisms
>   ■ Give examples of how different plants and animals have features that help them thrive in different kinds of places. Recognize that these features may be external or internal.

>   ■ Explore and illustrate that in both the short and long term (millions of years), changes in the environment have resulted in qualitative and quantitative changes in the species of plants and animals that inhabit the earth.

Preparation

- ❏ Copy questions and sketch sheets
- ❏ Copy flip book pages that are divided into thirds labeled *head, body, tail*
- ❏ Find pictures of climate regions

Materials

For each student
- ❏ 7 sheets of question/ sketching paper
- ❏ Pencil
- ❏ 7 sheets of white copy paper for final copies (8 1/2 x 11)
- ❏ 9 sheets of construction paper (8 1/2 x 11)

For class
- ❏ Pictures of climate regions and/or animals
- ❏ Markers/paint/crayons/colored pencils
- ❏ Scissors

Pre-project Discussion

- ■ Teach the concept of Pangaea and continent shifting.
- ■ Discuss how climate has a significant impact on adaptation and how creatures adapted as the continents drifted apart. Explain how this project is designed to mirror this type of evolution.
- ■ Explain that students will take one animal and adapt it to live successfully in seven different climate regions.
- ■ Describe seven climate regions (*grassland, tundra, swamp, rainforest, desert, mountain, ocean*), the types of animals and plants that live there, temperature, weather, and other features.
- ■ Use vocabulary words like *adaptation, habitat,* and *climate* throughout the discussion.
- ■ The amount of time required in the pre-project discussion will be determined by the degree of familiarity students have with animals and climate regions. You might want to consider reading them a book or showing a video if they have limited knowledge.

Procedure

1. Hand out questions and sketch sheets.

2. Students fill out one sheet for each climate area. They answer questions first so they start thinking about what characteristics their animal should have.

3. Students sketch their invented animals.

4. When they have all seven animals sketched, have them pick thier favorite five animals to enlarge and color on the 8 1/2 x 11 divided paper.

5. Before students draw large animals, make sure they understand concept of a flip book and that the animals' heads, bodies, and tails on each page need to line up for it to work.

6. When they are finished drawing their animals, students glue each page to an 8 1/2 x 11 sheet of construction paper (this will give them additional support so that they won't tear).

7. Students use two other pieces of construction paper to make front and back covers of book.

8. Bind pages into book form using a book-binder, staples, or paper fasteners. Make sure to bind books in a way that will stay together after pages are cut. The book's cover should help.

9. Once book is bound, students cut drawings along vertical dividing lines.

10. When students finish books, have them flip through, creating fantastic creatures through odd head-body-tail combinations.

Post Project Reflection

Ask students to share flipbooks with a friend and explain why they decided to give animals particular characteristics.

Trouble Spots

■ Some students will become nervous about the drawing component of the project because they feel that they cannot draw. They will need encouragement.

■ All students will need to be pressed to invent new animals instead of drawing animals that already exist. The more creative the kids can be with their drawings, the more they will get out of the exercise.

■ Binding the books can also be difficult.

Variations & Extensions

■ Make flipbooks of different numbers of animals.

■ Draw scenery behind animals on different pages to reinforce climate differences.

the **Pangaea Pete** FLIPBOOK

Picture Spot!

THE GAME

PANGAEA PETE IS AN ANIMAL WHO LIVES ON A CONTINENT ORIGINALLY PART OF THE PANGAEA SUPERCONTINENT 200 MILLION YEARS AGO. AS THE CONTINENTS DRIFT APART OVER MILLIONS OF YEARS, THE ENVIRONMENT CHANGES, AND PETE MUST ADAPT IN ORDER TO SURVIVE...

THIS IS HOW I PLAYED PANGAEA PETE (A PROCEDURE: USE WORDS LIKE "FIRST," "THEN," "NEXT"):_____
_____
_____

THE FLIPBOOK

BY USING THE FLIPBOOK, YOU CAN SEE HOW PETE HAD TO ADAPT TO SURVIVE IN DIFFERENT ENVIRONMENTS OR CLIMATES. THEN, YOU CAN MIX THEM UP TO CREATE CRAZY CREATURES! HERE ARE DEFINITIONS THAT YOU NEED TO KNOW TO USE THE PANGAEA PETE FLIPBOOK. I WROTE THEM IN MY OWN WORDS, USING COMPLETE SENTENCES!

ADAPTATION_____
ENVIRONMENT_____
HABITAT_____
CLIMATE_____
PANGAEA_____
CONTINENT_____

Pangaea Pete!

INVENT A CREATURE THAT LIVES IN THIS HABITAT. THESE QUESTIONS WILL HELP YOU THINK ABOUT YOUR CREATURE'S ADAPTATIONS.

HOW DOES THIS CREATURE MOVE?

_____

_____

WHAT DOES THIS CREATURE EAT?

_____

_____

HOW DOES THIS CREATURE CATCH ITS FOOD?

_____

_____

HOW DOES THIS CREATURE DEFEND ITSELF?

_____

_____

Name _____

Habitat _____

Sketch your creature HERE!

HEAD	BODY	TAIL

Boat Building

| DOMAIN OF SCIENCE: | **Physical Science** | Life Science | Earth Science |
| COMPLEXITY OF PREPARATION: | Low | **Medium** | High |

Every kid has seen a boat—whether on the ocean or on TV. Many urban students have never gotten to ride in one, and few have had the chance to think about just what makes them float and what makes them go. This activity gives students the chance to build their own boats and learn experimentally about how they work.

GOAL: USE MODEL BOATS TO EXPLORE QUALITIES OF FLOATING AND SINKING OBJECTS, TRANSFER OF ENERGY, AND MOTION

Objectives:

- Build a boat based on a model sailboat
- Identify differences between objects that sink and float
- Identify design features that facilitate motion in water
- Describe motion of objects
- Make and test scientific hypotheses concerning model boats

Estimated Time Line

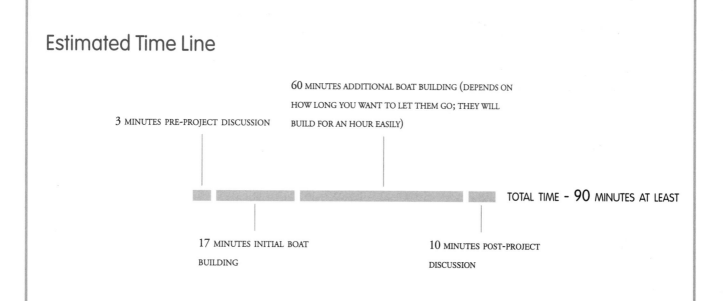

60 MINUTES ADDITIONAL BOAT BUILDING (DEPENDS ON HOW LONG YOU WANT TO LET THEM GO; THEY WILL BUILD FOR AN HOUR EASILY)

3 MINUTES PRE-PROJECT DISCUSSION

TOTAL TIME - **90** MINUTES AT LEAST

17 MINUTES INITIAL BOAT BUILDING

10 MINUTES POST-PROJECT DISCUSSION

Applicable Standards from the Massachusetts Science & Technology Frameworks

By its nature, every KidLab lesson addresses almost all of the elementary and middle school standards in Strand 1 (Inquiry) and Strand 3 (Technology) of the Science & Technology Frameworks. In addition, this lesson addresses the following standards in Strand 2 (Domains of Science, Physical Sciences):

- Position and Motion of Objects
  - Describe the motion of an object in terms of change in position relative to another object or the background.

- Motions and Changes in Motion
  - Show and describe how forces acting on objects as pushes or pulls can either reinforce or oppose each other.

Preparation

- ❑ Trace the shape of the boat on sheets of oaktag for each student to cut out.
- ❑ Cut straws in half.
- ❑ Cut sails and punch holes in the top and bottom of each sail.
- ❑ Make small balls of modeling clay.
- ❑ Devise some form of water surface.
- ❑ Get a fan.
- ❑ Build a boat to show the students as a model.

Materials

For class

The number of items that you need will depend on how many boats you want the children to make. If you are going to have them dismantle as they build they can reuse the modeling clay and straws.

For each boat

- ❑ Enough oaktag for the boat base (5-6 inches long and 2-3 inches wide)
- ❑ Aluminum foil to cover oaktag boat base
- ❑ 1/2 of a straw for each mast
- ❑ Small ball of modeling clay (1/2 inch diameter) to affix the straw to the oaktag
- ❑ White construction paper
- ❑ Scissors

For waterway

- ❑ Water table
- ❑ Fan

Pre-Project Discussion

A simple conversation about boats, what they look like, what they do, and what makes them special.

Procedure

1. Show the kids the model boat.
2. Students cut out the boat base from the oaktag. Have them start with an oval shape that comes to points at the ends.
3. Students cover bottom of base with aluminum foil and fold it up (1/2 inch) on the sides to make walls.
4. Students poke straw through 2 holes in construction paper sail.
5. Students attach straw to oaktag with modeling clay.
6. Set up fan at one end of waterway.
7. Test sail boats.
8. Allow students to try out other boat designs and see how they sail (this constitutes bulk of activity time).
9. Encourage students to reuse modeling clay, straws, and sails (if they aren't wet).

Post-Project Reflection

Use a large piece of paper and have the kids come up with a **RULES** sheet for successful floating and sailing boats. To guide the development of the rules sheet ask questions like:

What did you observe?
>Which boats sailed the best?
>How did the wind effect the boats?

Why did you make the decisions you made to alter your course?
>What designs did you try and what were the results?
>Why did you decide to make the changes that you made?

Compare one design to another: Which is more effective?
>What are the common characteristics of boats that floated and sailed the most successfully?

Example rules

- ■ If water gets in the boat it sinks.
- ■ You need to make the sides high enough or water gets in and the boat sinks.
- ■ The sail needs to face the correct way or the boat won't go.
- ■ A boat with a point in the front sails the best.
- ■ Square boats don't sail very well.

Trouble Spots

■ Some children will become upset when they experience the tragedy of a sinking boat. You will need to help them understand that it is okay when a boat sinks because it is a learning process.
■ Students sometimes also have difficulty controlling themselves with the water.

Variations & Extensions

■ Instead of a water table, a plastic file holder, fish tank, or another container will work to hold the water. It does not need to be deep, but should be at least 2 feet long.
■ Students can decorate sails to give boats more personality.

Cells

DOMAIN OF SCIENCE: Physical Science   **Life Science**   Earth Science
COMPLEXITY OF PREPARATION: Low   **Medium**   High

One of the hardest parts of science (and any learning) is turning abstract concepts that we can't see into concrete lessons. In this activity, kids turn microscopic cells into something they can see and touch. By using metaphors in their design (i.e., making the nucleus of the cell look like a brain or the mitochondria look like factories), students are also better able to remember the function behind what they have created. This approach—using hands-on construction to give form to the unseen world of science—is a mainstay of KidLab.

Objectives:

GOAL: MODEL THE PARTS OF A CELL TO UNDERSTAND CELLULAR PROCESSES

- Build a visual representation of cells and cell division
- Label parts of the cell and identify appropriate functions
- Explain the functions of parts of cells

Estimated Time Line

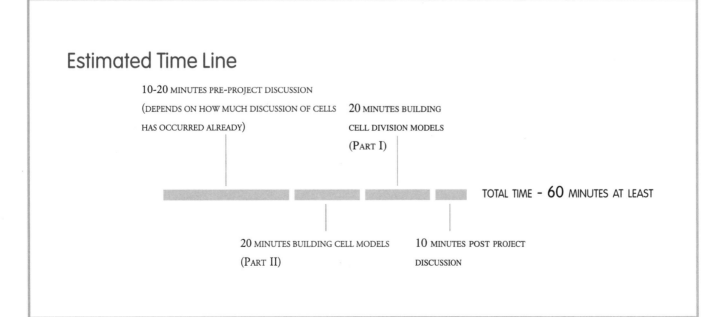

10-20 MINUTES PRE-PROJECT DISCUSSION (DEPENDS ON HOW MUCH DISCUSSION OF CELLS HAS OCCURRED ALREADY)

20 MINUTES BUILDING CELL DIVISION MODELS (PART I)

TOTAL TIME - **60** MINUTES AT LEAST

20 MINUTES BUILDING CELL MODELS (PART II)

10 MINUTES POST PROJECT DISCUSSION

Applicable Standards from the Massachusetts Science & Technology Frameworks

By its nature, every KidLab lesson addresses almost all of the elementary and middle school standards in Strand 1 (Inquiry) and Strand 3 (Technology) of the Science & Technology Frameworks. In addition, this lesson addresses the following standards in Strand 2 (Domains of Science, Life Sciences):

■ Identify the cell as the basic unit of life and the smallest unit that can reproduce itself. Give examples of single and multi-cellular organisms.

■ Observe and explain that in single cells there are common features that all cells have as well as differences that determine their function.

■ Investigate and illustrate evidence that cell replication results in multiplication of cells.

Preparation

❑ Get pictures of cells and cell division
❑ Make or buy playdough (if making playdough, there is a recipe on cornstarch boxes)

Materials

For class
PART I - The parts of a cell
❑ Pieces of foam
❑ Ribbon
❑ String
❑ Colored paper
❑ Glue

PART II - Modeling cellular division
❑ Playdough in different colors
❑ Toothpicks
❑ Paper for students to build their models on

Pre-Project Discussion

■ Discuss the parts of cells and their functions.
■ Discuss cell division.

Procedure

PART I - The parts of a cell

1. Have students look at pictures of cells.

2. Lead a discussion about the different parts of a cell and their functions.

3. Have students choose different materials to make the different parts of the cell and build their own cells.

4. On an index card have students write the different parts of the cell and their functions.

PART II - Modeling cellular division

1. Have students look at pictures of cellular division.

2. Lead a discussion about cellular division.

3. Have students build models representing the four stages of cellular division. Students create each stage separately (using clay and toothpicks to represent chromosomes).

Post-Project Reflection

Have students explain their models to a partner.

Trouble Spots

■ Sometimes kids want to play with the playdough instead of modeling with it.

Variations & Extensions

■ Instead of having students build cells whose parts look like the real parts, have them build a cell whose parts look like the function. (e.g., nucleus as brain, mitochondria as factories)

The Little Things

DOMAIN OF SCIENCE: **Physical Science**   Life Science   Earth Science
COMPLEXITY OF PREPARATION: Low   **Medium**   High

One of the hardest parts of science (and any learning) is turning abstract concepts that we can't see into concrete lessons. Sculptures of molecules are the quintessential response to this challenge. By combining chromatography with molecules, this lesson helps kids explore the concept of the "little things" that we can't see, but that are hiding inside all the bigger things that we use everyday and give them unique characteristics. This becomes a valuable lesson for understanding a variety of other concepts—scientific and otherwise.

Objectives:

GOAL: USE CHROMATOGRAPHY AND MODEL MOLECULES TO UNDERSTAND AND ILLUSTRATE THAT OBJECTS ARE MADE UP OF SMALLER PARTS THAT WE CANNOT SEE

■ Conduct chromatography experiment and identify different combinations of inks that constitute different black markers

■ Define concept of molecule and atom

■ Identify that all matter is made up of molecules, and molecules are made up of atoms

■ Create models of simple molecules, identifying atoms that make up each molecule

Estimated Time Line

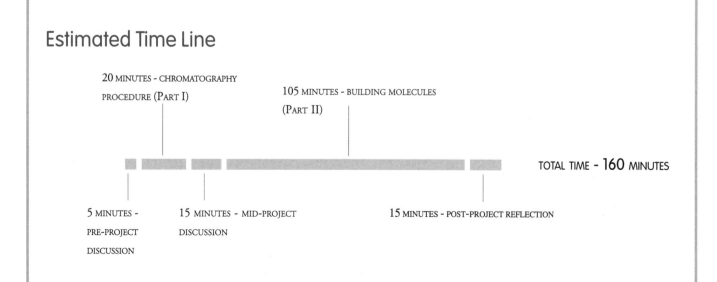

20 MINUTES - CHROMATOGRAPHY PROCEDURE (PART I)

105 MINUTES - BUILDING MOLECULES (PART II)

TOTAL TIME - **160** MINUTES

5 MINUTES - PRE-PROJECT DISCUSSION

15 MINUTES - MID-PROJECT DISCUSSION

15 MINUTES - POST-PROJECT REFLECTION

Applicable Standards from the Massachusetts Science & Technology Frameworks

By its nature, every KidLab lesson addresses almost all of the elementary and middle school standards in Strand 1 (Inquiry) and Strand 3 (Technology) of the Science & Technology Frameworks. In addition, this lesson addresses the following standards in Strand 2 (Domains of Science, Physical Sciences):

Properties of Matter

■ Give evidence that objects are made up of different materials.

■ Recognize and explain how experimental evidence supports the idea that matter can be viewed as composed of very small particles (such as atoms, molecules and ions).

Materials

PART 1: **Chromatography**

For each student
- ❏ Coffee filter
- ❏ Black, non-permanent marker (different brands for different students)
- ❏ Scissors
- ❏ Small piece of tape
- ❏ Pencil
- ❏ Cup of water
- ❏ Colored pencils

PART 2: **Molecule Building**

For each molecule
- ❏ Foam pieces in varying sizes
- ❏ Toothpicks

Preparation

- ❏ Find molecular formulas for six relatively simple molecules
- ❏ Construct model of water molecule out of toothpicks and foam

Pre Project Discussion

Brief discussion about the fact that matter is made up of smaller components that we cannot see.

Procedure

PART 1: **Chromatography**

1. Hand out *Discovering the Parts of a Substance* sheet.
2. Give each student a black, non-permanent marker. Different brands will yield different results. Scented markers have the widest color range results, so they are good to use.
3. Students cut a rectangle out of their coffee filter. To make this easier, give students a drawing of a 1" x 3" rectangle, which they can trace and then cut out.
4. With their black markers, students draw a line on the coffee filter.
5. Students tape coffee filter to pencil.

6. Students fill a paper cup one-quarter full of water.

7. Students lay the pencil across the top of the paper cup and place the filter hanging into the water. The black line must be above the water line.

8. As the homemade chromatography paper separates black ink into its constituent parts, students observe what is happening. They should then sketch the results in color.

PART 2: Building Molecules

1. Hand out toothpicks and foam pieces to students.

2. Explain that each piece of foam represents one atom and toothpicks will be used to bind atoms together to make molecules.

3. Present model of water molecule.

4. Each student constructs a water molecule. Use the same type of foam pieces for the same elements and different types for different elements (this helps students understand that all hydrogen atoms are the same and different from oxygen atoms).

5. Write six molecular formulas on the board and have the students try to build them. Remind them to use the same type of foam for the same elements throughout all of their molecules.

Post-Project Reflection

Have students pick their favorite molecule to present to the class, saying the molecule's formula, naming its atoms (letters and element names), and pointing to them.

Trouble Spots

■ You will need enough foam pieces that look alike and enough different types of foam for students to build molecules.

■ Molecules can become large and unwieldy. To control the size of molecules, give students a board or piece of paper to use as a construction base.

Variations & Extensions

■ Instead of using the chromatography procedure, break something else into its parts (e.g., milk into curds and whey).

■ Make the molecular formulas more difficult or make some challenge molecules.

■ Use gumdrops and marshmallows or pieces of colored Styrofoam instead of foam pieces for atoms.

■ Use the periodic table and have students look at the atomic mass of the atoms to pick an appropriate size of foam to represent the relative size of the atoms.

■ Have students glue some molecules to pieces of paper and write their molecular formula and element names on the paper.

■ Have students find the elements on the periodic table.

■ Use books with drawings or photographs of molecules, atoms, crystals, etc. for students to look at.

Discovering the Parts of a Substance!

THIS TEST IS CALLED *CHROMATOGRAPHY*. SCIENTISTS USE THIS TEST TO FIND OUT WHAT A SUBSTANCE, LIKE INK OR LIPSTICK, IS MADE OF. OFTEN, THINGS THAT LOOK THE SAME ARE ACTUALLY MADE OF DIFFERENT CHEMICAL PARTS.

PROCEDURE

1. TRACE THE EXAMPLE BELOW ONTO YOUR COFFEE FILTER, AND CUT IT OUT.
2. USE YOUR BLACK MARKER TO DRAW A LINE JUST LIKE ON THE EXAMPLE.
3. TAPE YOUR RECTANGLE ONTO THE PENCIL.
4. PLACE THE FILTER INTO THE WATER, WITH THE PENCIL ON TOP OF THE CUP.
5. *OBSERVE* WHAT HAPPENS.
6. SKETCH YOUR RESULTS IN *COLOR* ON THE EXAMPLE BELOW.

WHILE YOU ARE WAITING, ANSWER THESE QUESTIONS:

_____
_____
_____
_____
_____
_____
_____

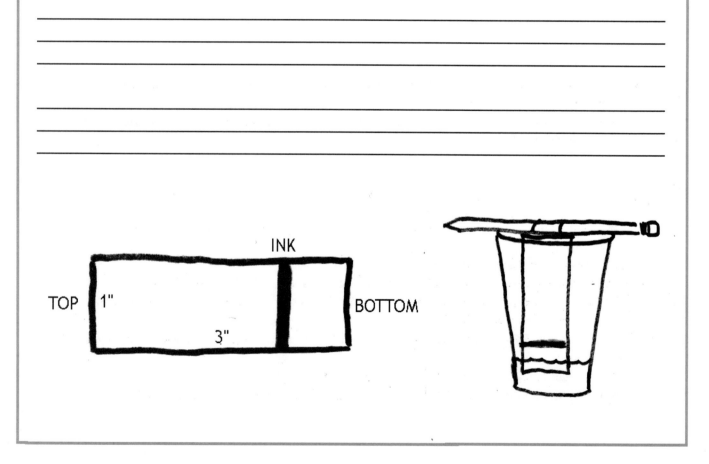

The Earth and its Properties

DOMAIN OF SCIENCE:	Physical Science	Life Science	**Earth Science**
COMPLEXITY OF PREPARATION:	**Low**	Medium	High

One of the hardest parts of science (and any learning) is turning abstract concepts that we can't see into concrete lessons. In this activity, kids delve beneath the Earth's surface to understand what our planet is made of. This approach—using hands-on construction to give form to the unseen world of science—is a mainstay of KidLab.

GOAL: BUILD GEODOMES TO REPRESENT THE EARTH AND ITS LAYERS

Objectives:

- ■ Use various materials to build representation of earth core
- ■ Reproduce forms that reflect structure of plates, islands, mountain ranges, and other features formed by earth layers
- ■ Demonstrate understanding that earth is made up of three layers and that features are formed by plate tectonics

Estimated Time Line with Suggested Stopping Points

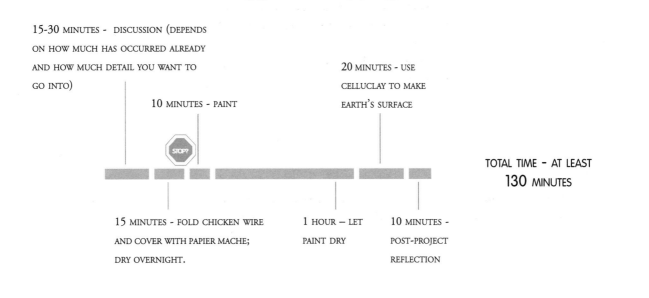

15-30 MINUTES - DISCUSSION (DEPENDS ON HOW MUCH HAS OCCURRED ALREADY AND HOW MUCH DETAIL YOU WANT TO GO INTO)

10 MINUTES - PAINT

20 MINUTES - USE CELLUCLAY TO MAKE EARTH'S SURFACE

TOTAL TIME - AT LEAST **130** MINUTES

15 MINUTES - FOLD CHICKEN WIRE AND COVER WITH PAPIER MACHE; DRY OVERNIGHT.

1 HOUR – LET PAINT DRY

10 MINUTES - POST-PROJECT REFLECTION

Applicable Standards from the Massachusetts Science & Technology Frameworks

By its nature, every KidLab lesson addresses almost all of the elementary and middle school standards in Strand 1 (Inquiry) and Strand 3 (Technology) of the Science & Technology Frameworks. In addition, this lesson addresses the following standards in Strand 2 (Domains of Science, Earth Sciences):

■ Demonstrate an understanding of the internal and external structure of the planet Earth

■ Illustrate that the interior of the earth is hot. Heat flow and movement of material within the Earth moves the continents, causes earthquakes and volcanic eruptions, and creates mountains and ocean basins.

Preparation

❑ Cut pieces of chicken wire into 2 ft by 2 ft squares
❑ Make papier-mâché
❑ Put celluclay into 3 different containers and use food coloring dye one green, one blue, and one brown.

Materials

For class
❑ Chicken wire
❑ Papier-mâché
❑ Paint
❑ Celluclay or finely cut papier-mâché (this can be bought in craft stores or made by putting newspaper into a blender and then mixing it with glue)
❑ Food coloring
❑ Images of Earth and its layers from a science textbook or atlas

Pre Project discussion

Discussion of continental plates, oceanic plates, mountain ranges, islands, and the three layers of the earth (core, mantle, and crust). Teachers can also include a discussion of plate tectonics.

Procedure

1. Give each student a piece of chicken wire
2. Teacher fold chicken wire into half circle
3. Students cover half circles of chicken wire with papier-mâché and let dry
4. Students paint inside of dome to reflect three layers of earth and let dry
5. Students use celluclay to create continental plates (thick clay), oceanic plates (thin clay), islands, and mountain ranges on the outside of the dome and let dry

Post Project Discussion

Have students look at actual representations of the Earth and compare this to their models. What do they see in their models? What features does the Earth diagram have that they don't see in their models?

Trouble Spots

■ Papier-mâché and celluclay can be messy.
■ You will need to have something planned for students to do while projects are drying at various stages.

Variations and Extensions

■ You could model the plates and elevations using a flat model instead of the dome
■ Students can model actual continental plates, oceanic plates, mountain ranges, and islands or make them up understanding the concepts.

Erosion

DOMAIN OF SCIENCE:	Physical Science	Life Science	**Earth Science**
COMPLEXITY OF PREPARATION:	Low	**Medium**	High

Erosion is one of those scientific concepts that is not, on its own, very exciting to students. By turning an erosion lesson into an elaborate, hands-on experiment, KidLab makes it fun. Experimenting with dirt and soil and water, learning about erosion becomes another fun challenge of the KidLab classroom.

GOAL: TO USE A MODEL RIVERBED TO ILLUSTRATE AND UNDERSTAND HOW EROSION WORKS

Objectives:

■ Construct a model riverbed out of various materials
■ Observe and record the effect of water on sand, soil, and other items in model riverbed
■ Make and test hypotheses about erosion and how it works

Estimated Time Line with Suggested Stopping Point

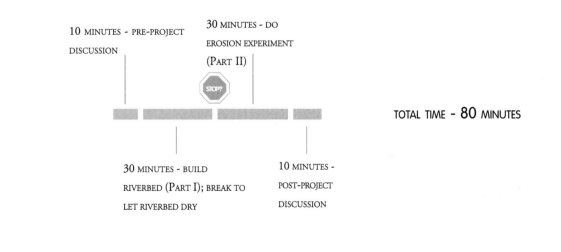

10 MINUTES - PRE-PROJECT DISCUSSION

30 MINUTES - DO EROSION EXPERIMENT (PART II)

STOP?

30 MINUTES - BUILD RIVERBED (PART I); BREAK TO LET RIVERBED DRY

10 MINUTES - POST-PROJECT DISCUSSION

TOTAL TIME - **80** MINUTES

Applicable Standards from the Massachusetts Science & Technology Frameworks

By its nature, every KidLab lesson addresses almost all of the elementary and middle school standards in Strand 1 (Inquiry) and Strand 3 (Technology) of the Science & Technology Frameworks. In addition, this lesson addresses the following standards in Strand 2 (Domains of Science, Earth Sciences):

Properties and Changes of Earth's Materials

■ Illustrate that the Earth's surface is composed of water, rocks, soils, and living organisms

■ Show evidence that water flows downhill in streams and rivers

Materials

For each student
❑ 1 piece of oaktag 2 feet long and 8 inches wide
❑ 1 piece of aluminum foil large enough to cover oaktag
❑ 4-5 rocks
❑ 1 plastic cup
❑ 3-4 popsicle sticks
❑ Piece of paper to record data

For class
❑ Water
❑ Sand
❑ Soil
❑ Gravel
❑ Dirt with grass growing on it
❑ Plaster of paris
❑ Tape

Preparation

❑ Mix plaster of paris

❑ Cut oaktag into pieces that are 2 feet long and 8 inches wide

❑ Make a model for the kids to look at.

Pre-Project Discussion

Ask students questions that illustrate everyday examples of erosion. For instance:

■ What do you see happening to the rain on the ground when it rains?

■ Has anyone built a sandcastle by the ocean? What happens to it when the water comes in?

■ Has anyone ever seen the Grand Canyon?

Procedure

PART 1

1. Hand out a piece of oaktag, some popsicle sticks, and a few rocks to each student.

2. Have students fold up long sides to create two-inch-high walls.

3. Students then cover oaktag with tin foil.

4. Pour plaster of paris into the oaktage to form the riverbed.

5. While the plaster of paris is still wet have students place a few rocks into it and stick popsicle sticks vertically into it (to simulate trees).

6. Leave riverbed to harden (probably overnight or at least for a few hours).

7. Give each student a plastic cup and have them punch a hole the diameter of a pencil width in the bottom (this hole will help control the flow of water).

PART 2

8. Go outside with riverbeds, water, plastic cups, sand, soil, gravel, dirt with grass growing on it, a few buckets of water, and recording sheet.

9. Have students cover riverbeds with sand.

10. Students fill cups with water, hold riverbed at an angle, and hold cup over elevated end.

11. When cup is empty, have students look at results and draw picture of riverbed on recording sheet.

12. Repeat with other ground coverings.

13. Students can also experiment holding riverbed at varying angles with same ground covering to compare what happens.

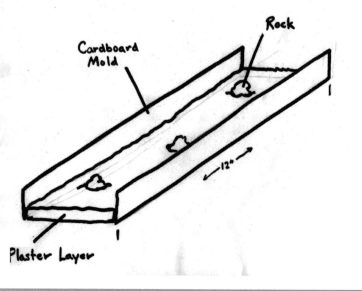

Plaster Riverbed Mold

Rock

Cardboard Mold

~12"

Plaster Layer

Post-Project Reflection

What did you observe?

■ How did the different soils erode?

Compare to one design to another:

■ Which is more effective?

■ What would happen if you built on the different surfaces?

■ Have students look at different photographs and try to guess how they would erode.

Trouble Spots

■ Both the plaster of paris and the erosion process can become messy. If you can do the erosion outside it will be easier.

■ The experiment also requires a lot of water.

■ The plaster of paris riverbeds sometimes crack, which can upset the kids.

Example rules

■ If water gets in the boat it sinks.

■ You need to make the sides high enough or water gets in and the boat sinks.

■ The sail needs to face the correct way or the boat won't go.

■ A boat with a point in the front sails the best.

■ Square boats don't sail very well.

Variations & Extensions

■ Instead of having each student make his or her own riverbed you can make one large riverbed and the whole class can work together.

■ The erosion component can be done inside using buckets to collect the runoff.

■ You do not need to cover the oaktag and tinfoil with plaster of paris if you do not what to. Using the aluminum foil surface will work (you can even glue the rocks and popsicle sticks down with a hot glue gun), but the plaster of paris creates a more realistic ground covering.

WHAT IS THE RIVERBED COVERED WITH?

NAME

SKETCH HOW YOUR RIVERBED LOOKS
AFTER YOU RUN THE WATER.

Looking Inside the Human Body

DOMAIN OF SCIENCE: Physical Science **Life Science** Earth Science
COMPLEXITY OF PREPARATION: **Low** Medium High

When we learn about the many organs that make up the human body, it is easy to lose sight of the fact that these make up *our* bodies. This activity helps bring home the fact that science is not an abstraction far away from us, but is actually about understanding ourselves.

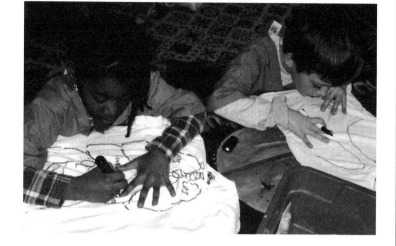

GOAL: FAMILIARIZE STUDENTS WITH THE CONCEPT AND FUNCTION OF HUMAN ORGANS

Objectives:

■ Trace front and back organs on representation of human body
■ Review functions of organs
■ Explore how different organs work together and functions interact

Estimated Time Line with Suggested Stopping Points

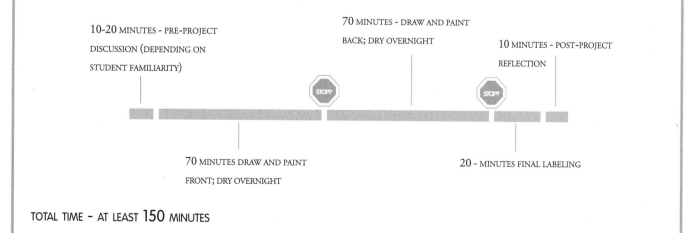

10-20 MINUTES - PRE-PROJECT DISCUSSION (DEPENDING ON STUDENT FAMILIARITY)

70 MINUTES - DRAW AND PAINT BACK; DRY OVERNIGHT

10 MINUTES - POST-PROJECT REFLECTION

70 MINUTES DRAW AND PAINT FRONT; DRY OVERNIGHT

20 - MINUTES FINAL LABELING

TOTAL TIME - AT LEAST **150** MINUTES

Applicable Standards from the Massachusetts Science & Technology Frameworks

By its nature, every KidLab lesson addresses almost all of the elementary and middle school standards in Strand 1 (Inquiry) and Strand 3 (Technology) of the Science & Technology Frameworks. In addition, this lesson addresses the following standards in Strand 2 (Domains of Science, Life Sciences):

■ Investigate and explain that complex multi-cellular organisms are interacting systems of cells, tissues, and organs that fulfill life processes through mechanical, electrical, and chemical means, including procuring or manufacturing food, breathing, and respiration.

Preparation

❑ Copy a picture of the organ drawings for each student
❑ Cut pieces of cardboard so that they are at least the same size as the legal paper

Materials

For class
❑ Legal-size paper with front organs (heart, lungs, gallbladder, liver, stomach, intestines, etc.)
❑ Legal-size paper with back bones and organs (kidney, spine, ribs, pelvis, scapula)
❑ 1 white T-shirt for each student
❑ Black permanent marker
❑ 1 piece of cardboard for each student
❑ Many colors of paint
❑ Paper clips

Pre-Project Discussion

Discuss the different organs in the human body and their locations and functions.

Procedure

1. Hand out copies of organ drawings.
2. Students tape drawings to piece of cardboard, slide cardboard into T-shirt so that drawing aligns with shirt appropriately, and paperclip cardboard in place.
3. Using permanent black markers, students trace front organs onto T-shirt.
4. Students remove paper from cardboard, leaving cardboard in T-shirt so that paint does not run.
5. Students paint each organ in a different color.
6. Allow shirts to dry overnight.
7. Repeat steps 3-5 for back of T-shirt.
8. When entire T-shirt is dry, label each organ with black permanent marker.

Post-Project Reflection

Students look at one another's shirts. Ask students to show rest of class their shirts and explain how they colored them.

Trouble Spots

■ Painting can get messy.
■ You might want to have students bring in T-shirts a few days before so that if they forget them the first day, they will have them in time to work on them.

Variations & Extensions

■ Students can make only the front or only the back instead of both.
■ Students can use fabric pens instead of paint.

Mini Golf

DOMAIN OF SCIENCE:	Physical Science	Life Science	Earth Science
COMPLEXITY OF PREPARATION:	Low	Medium	High

Part of the fun of KidLab is making games that you can play. When kids build a mini-golf course, they get to do just that. Similar experiments (not included in this booklet) allow kids to build model roadways, board games, and racetracks. As they build and play the games, they get to test the scientific principles that make the game work.

GOAL: LEARN ABOUT MOTION AND TRANSFER OF ENERGY THROUGH MINI-GOLF

Objectives:

■ Build a mini-golf course using available materials
■ Make and test hypotheses concerning movement of the ball
■ Demonstrate understanding of notions of force, direction, speed, and velocity
■ Demonstrate understanding that different materials absorb energy in different ways and affect motion as a result

Estimated Time Line with Suggested Stopping Points

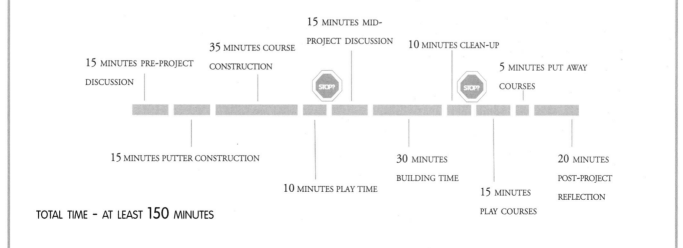

15 MINUTES PRE-PROJECT DISCUSSION

35 MINUTES COURSE CONSTRUCTION

15 MINUTES MID-PROJECT DISCUSSION

10 MINUTES CLEAN-UP

5 MINUTES PUT AWAY COURSES

15 MINUTES PUTTER CONSTRUCTION

10 MINUTES PLAY TIME

30 MINUTES BUILDING TIME

15 MINUTES PLAY COURSES

20 MINUTES POST-PROJECT REFLECTION

TOTAL TIME – AT LEAST 150 MINUTES

Applicable Standards from the Massachusetts Science & Technology Frameworks

By its nature, every KidLab lesson addresses almost all of the elementary and middle school standards in Strand 1 (Inquiry) and Strand 3 (Technology) of the Science & Technology Frameworks. In addition, this lesson addresses the following standards in Strand 2 (Domains of Science, Physical Sciences):

Position and Motion of Objects
- Experience and describe how an object's motion can be changed through the action of a push or pull on the object.

Motions and Changes in Motion
- Demonstrate that all forces have magnitude and direction.

Preparation

Make model course and model putter
- The course can have objects glued on **top** of the cardboard or on the **bottom** so that they create hills and obstacles.
- Try your course before showing it to the kids to make sure that it works.
- Make the course a level of complexity that is appropriate for your age students.

Materials

For each student
- Piece of cardboard or oaktag 36"x24" with a traced hole at one end (students will cut this out to serve as their golf hole)
- Wooden dowel 36" long by ½" diameter (for putter handle)
- Foam rectangle 4"x1"x1" (for putter)
- Ping pong ball

For class
- Miscellaneous pieces of cardboard, foam, paper towel tubes, and other materials that can serve as obstacles
- Glue or hot glue
- Tape
- Scissors

Pre-Project Discussion

- Discuss what golf and mini golf are.
- Show sample course.

Procedure

Part 1 - Putter Construction

1. Each student glues rectangular piece of foam to end of dowel.
2. Each student gets ping pong ball and tests putter.

Part 2 - Course Construction

1. Each student gets a piece of cardboard with a hole drawn on it and cuts out the hole.
2. Students glue or tape objects on their piece of cardboard. Encourage them to periodically test their courses with their ping pong ball to see how they are working.
3. Students break from working to play one another's unfinished courses.
4. Bring students together to discuss what types of courses and structures work well to guide ball to hole.
5. Students return to working on courses, incorporating ideas from discussion.
6. (Optional) Students who finish early can paint courses.
7. Students play one another's finished courses.
8. Time permitting, students can alter courses based on lessons after playing rounds.

Post-Project Reflection

Students come up with a **RULES of the BALL** sheet. To guide the development of the rules sheet, focus on the movement of the ball and ask questions like:

What did you observe?
- What happened when you played?
- Describe the movement of the ball.
- How did you make the ball go in the hole?
- What made the ball do what it did? Why?

Why did you make the decisions you made to alter your course?
- What components worked well to get the ball into the hole?

Compare to one another: Which is more effective?
- Which designs were the most fun to play? Why?
- What qualities did the courses that worked well have in common?

Example rules:

- The ball can't move itself.
- The harder you hit the ball, the faster it goes.
- The mini golf course told the ball where to go.
- Sides keep the ball on track.
- The ball only changes direction if it hits something or if the bottom is uneven.
- You have to hit the ball harder to make it go uphill than to make it go downhill.

Trouble Spots

- The most common trouble spot occurs in the pre-project discussion about mini-golf. Many students have never played mini-golf and have no familiarity with what courses look like. Therefore, the pre project discussion must be fairly comprehensive. You might want to show students pictures of mini-golf courses or get a mini-golf CD-ROM game.

Variations & Extensions

- Courses can be more or less complicated
- Larger piece of cardboard for more elaborate holes
- More conversation with clearer descriptions of ball behavior
- Use new vocabulary (force, friction, gravity)
- Have students write an observation sheet after playing courses and before discussion

Natural Disaster

DOMAIN OF SCIENCE:	Physical Science	Life Science	**Earth Science**
COMPLEXITY OF PREPARATION:	Low	Medium	**High**

The baking soda-and-vinegar volcano is a staple of every American's science fair childhood. This experiment takes that age-old experiment one step further, creating a fun activity for kids to think about the impact that natural phenomena have on people's lives.

GOAL: TO CREATE A NEWS STORY ABOUT A VOLCANIC ERUPTION IN ORDER TO EXPLORE THE RELATIONSHIP BETWEEN SCIENCE AND HUMAN AFFAIRS

Objectives:

■ Use household items to create a model volcano

■ Learn about the roles of various scientists—such as meteorologists and seismologists—in understanding and predicting natural phenomena

■ Use performance to explore the impact of volcanoes on human affairs

Estimated Time Line with Suggested Stopping Points

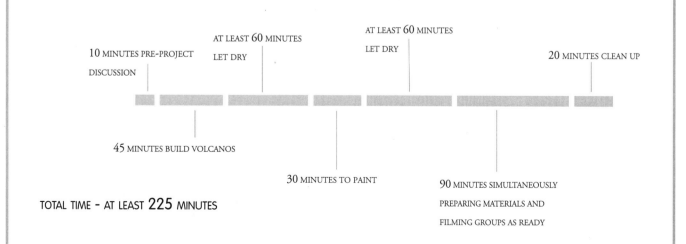

10 MINUTES PRE-PROJECT DISCUSSION

AT LEAST 60 MINUTES LET DRY

AT LEAST 60 MINUTES LET DRY

20 MINUTES CLEAN UP

45 MINUTES BUILD VOLCANOS

30 MINUTES TO PAINT

90 MINUTES SIMULTANEOUSLY PREPARING MATERIALS AND FILMING GROUPS AS READY

TOTAL TIME - AT LEAST 225 MINUTES

Applicable Standards from the Massachusetts Science & Technology Frameworks

By its nature, every KidLab lesson addresses almost all of the elementary and middle school standards in Strand 1 (Inquiry) and Strand 3 (Technology) of the Science & Technology Frameworks. In addition, this lesson addresses the following standards in Strand 2 (Domains of Science, Physical Sciences):

■ Examine and demonstrate evidence that weather can be studied in terms of properties of the atmosphere such as pressure, temperature, humidity, wind speed and direction, precipitation, and the amount and type of clouds.

■ Illustrate that the interior of the Earth is hot. Heat flow and movement of material within the Earth move the continents, cause earthquakes and volcanic eruptions, and create mountains and ocean basins

Preparation

This activity requires a script for a news program describing the volcanic eruption and its impact. You can write the script based on a 4-5 minute lecture that you would give on the subject. The script could include:

❑ Roles for a newscaster, meteorologist, seismologist, and townspeople.

❑ A newscaster who introduces the story

❑ A studio meteorologist who uses maps to explain what is happening

❑ A field reporter who interviews scientists and townspeople on location

❑ A meteorologist and seismologist on location who report different warning signs of a volcanic eruption.

❑ Local residents who get to run screaming from the volcano and discuss its impact on their lives and livelihoods.

Materials

For volcano
❑ Chicken wire
❑ Papier-mâché
❑ Paint
❑ Baking soda
❑ Vinegar
❑ Red food coloring
❑ Paper cup

For news story
❑ News script
❑ Video camera
❑ Sample weather maps showing temperature and precipitation
❑ Sample satellite maps
❑ Crayons, markers, or colored pencils
❑ Paper

Pre-Project Discussion

■ Prior to the activity, have students watch the news and weather reports.

■ Discuss what features make up a good weather report and why we have weather reports.

■ Explain to the students that they are going to create and film a news story about a volcanic eruption on a tropical island.

Procedure

Part 1: The Eruption

1. Bend chicken wire into a volcano shape.

2. Put a paper cup into top part of the volcano where the eruption will come from.

3. Cover volcano with papier maché and let dry.

4. Paint volcano green/brown.

5. Fill the paper cup half full with baking soda.

6. In a separate bottle, mix vinegar with red food coloring

Part 2: The News

1. Students break into different roles

   ■ Some students have parts in the newscast. These students should rehearse their roles.

   ■ Some students create precipitation maps, temperature maps, and satellite maps of the area.

   ■ Some students construct a small model village around the base of the volcano to be destroyed by the volcano.

   ■ The teacher is the cinematographer for the production

2. When materials are ready, begin filming script.

3. Mix vinegar and baking soda for volcano to erupt at appropriate point in newscast.

Post-Project Reflection

Watch the news story and share it with another class of students.

Trouble Spots

■ Students sometimes will get carried away with ideas for scenes that they will want to include in the film.

■ Students might get upset because more than one child wants a given part.

Variations & Extensions

■ Any alterations can be made in the script ideas presented here.